What Will Happen to God?

What Will Happen to God?

Feminism and the Reconstruction of Christian Belief

William Oddie

IGNATIUS PRESS   SAN FRANCISCO

First English Edition
© 1984, SPCK, London

Published with the assistance of
The Evangelical and Catholic Mission
McLean, Virginia

Cover design by Riz Boncan Marsella

Cover illustration; "Christa", a sculpture by Edwina Sandys,
reproduced by permission of the artist

This book is dedicated
with love to
THE FEMALE SEX,
particularly to
my mother, my wife and my daughters,
and to
THE GLORY OF GOD
THE FATHER

Contents

WHAT WILL HAPPEN TO GOD? I first asked myself this question in 1971. I was sitting in a circle of women in Westchester, New York. We were all 'housewives' with families and homes to care for. Some of us worked outside the home as well. It was the first consciousness-raising group I had ever attended.

Naomi Goldenberg, *Changing of the Gods*

Foreword to the American Edition

The American edition of *What Will Happen to God?* appears at a time of turmoil and confusion for the Christian cause, in North America perhaps even more than in the rest of the Western World. It is a time of profound internal divisions, divisions which have deepened during the seventies and eighties within existing denominations rather than between them. And these divisions are opening up, not only among Episcopalians, Methodists and Lutherans, among Christians traditionally described (with varying degrees of accuracy) as "Protestant", but also, in America, between Roman Catholics.

This last development has brought disorientation, not only for the Roman Catholic Church in North America, but also for many non-Catholics, who (whatever their reservations) have always in their heart of hearts looked to Rome as the centre of Christendom's ultimate unity and as a guarantor of the objective character of the Christian revelation. The depth of this new schism, transcending all Western Christendom's historic boundaries, is now beginning to be apparent. For many conservatives, the extent of the revolution that is facing them is only now becoming clear. For liberal modernists, the extent of the resistance (hitherto often dormant) to their ambitions for the Church is also emerging. The Pope may, during his pastoral visit to the U.S.A. in 1987, have faced hostile demonstrations from radical Catholics (including radical feminists); but he also received the warm support of many times their number.

Whatever its real grassroots support, nevertheless, the revolution is still being waged, and its effects have often gone much further than many of those who launched it intended, further, indeed, than some of them have even now realised. Nowhere is this more true than in the Episcopal Church of the U.S.A., and nowhere has the practical effect of radical feminist theology as the revolution's most effective ideological weapon been more profound. In 1976, as the General Convention of ECUSA voted (by the narrowest of margins) for the ordination of women to the priesthood, Robert Terwilliger (then suffragan bishop of the Episcopal Diocese of Dallas) suggested that it might be the historic vocation of the Episcopal Church to show the rest of Catholic Christendom how profound were the dangers of this step. Twelve years later, his words have come true: the ordination of women priests in ECUSA has brought about, not a reform of the ordained ministry but an ecclesiological and theological revolution. It is a revolution which has only just begun to show itself. In the frank words of one of the successful revolutionaries, John Shelby Spong, bishop of Newark, New Jersey, "the liberals tend to see the women's movement . . . primarily in terms of justice and human rights. That is too shallow a judgment in my view. The conservatives, on the other hand, see the women's movement as a fundamental break with history and tradition. . . . They recognise . . . that much of what we Christians think of as crucial to the life of the Church will not survive the revolution. *They are correct*" [my italics].

One such liberal (David L. Edwards, Provost of Southwark), reviewing this book's English editions, objected that in its author's "entirely justified alarm about the more extreme expressions of Christian feminism . . . he has attached too much importance to them". Until now, it has been possible for liberals like Provost Edwards to fail to see how normal such "extreme expressions" have become. This is no longer possible within ECUSA, except for those who *will* not see. With the publication of an unassuming small volume, bound in black paper covers and demurely entitled "liturgical texts for evaluation", this comfortable myopia can no longer be sustained. It was published in 1987 by ECUSA's official standing liturgical commission; it, or some version of it, will almost certainly be authorised for general use.

The aims of these liturgies have been officially stated in a useful accompanying paper and in a "leader's manual"; there is little need for speculation as to what is intended. For the author of this book the contents of these documents are all too familiar. What has changed are the auspices under which these ideas are offered to the Church. No longer are they the *samizdat* of "extreme" Christian feminism; now, they are disseminated from the very heart of the Episcopalian Establishment. The aims of "liturgical texts for evaluation" are several; they are, *inter alia*, to go as far as possible towards phasing out the New Testament perception of God as "Father" and of Jesus as being his Son, and to installing a liturgy based as nearly as possible on radical feminist norms, as can be achieved without the man and woman in the pew actually realising what is going on. Once a new generation has been brought up on the "Black Mass Book" (as its opponents are calling it) ECUSA will be ready for the revolution's final stage. "The time may come", as the *Leader's Manual* puts it, "when, by using the images of this rite in prayer, another generation may well sufficiently reform and renew the perceptions and images of God actually to call God 'Mother' without hurting and alienating many faithful people". The "Black Mass Book", in fact, sets the official seal of approval on the radical feminist liturgies examined in part two of this study, and is itself a step towards the general implementation of the norms they exemplify. *Liturgical texts for evaluation* and its accompanying documents are indispensible reading for anyone seeking to understand the political and theological ideas underlying the revolution of which Bishop Spong writes.

It is the purpose of this book to examine the ideological assumptions of those (mostly from North America) who have not only brought ECUSA to this stage of its development, but whose followers are working tirelessly in other churches and in other lands to achieve the same result. Though the first edition appeared as recently as 1984, its conclusions—not only about the effect of large numbers of women priests on the Church's life and belief, but also about the revolutionary (and non-Christian) nature of much feminist theology, are, I believe, already being vindicated. As I write, events are unfolding which may well take ECUSA down the path it has chosen beyond the point of no return. For others, it is still not too late to draw back.

William Oddie

Introduction

This is not a book about the ordination of women to the priesthood, though as will become obvious enough, this is a question which can hardly be avoided by anyone seeking to understand the aims and influence of the modern feminist movement within western Christendom. An all-male priesthood presents an obvious target for Christian feminists; and radical feminism has always needed specific issues and campaigns to give coherence to a movement which tends to avoid structure and organization.

But the question of whether or not women can or ought to be priests poses another, which becomes in the end even more insistent: why should a practice which has, in the almost wistful words of a Vatican declaration, for so many centuries 'enjoyed peaceful and universal acceptance', so quickly have become so hotly contested; and what are the implications for Christian belief that it has?

For it is quite clear that very much more than a change in the ministry of the Church is at stake here. The controversy has arisen in those Churches which (unlike Protestant communities) retain a ministerial priesthood in which, as C. S. Lewis put it writing as an Anglican, 'the priest is a double representative, who represents us to God and God to us'. And it is beginning to be increasingly apparent - as the 'women's movement' within the Church comes to clarify its ambitions and even to begin to achieve them - that the problem has less to do with the Church's understanding of ministry, important though that is, than with its understanding (and at the most profound level) of the nature of man and the nature of God himself.

It is necessary to move beyond the immediate issues thrown up by the controversy surrounding women's ordination for more than one reason. Partly because it concentrates attention on one particular feminist objective in a way which tends to divide Reformed or Protestant Christians from those holding a more traditionally Catholic theology of ministry, a way which makes feminism appear more threatening to a Catholic than to a Protestant understanding of the Christian tradition. This view is certainly held by many at both ends of the broad spectrum of opinion within my own Anglican communion. For this reason, I have not written at any length on feminist attitudes to the Blessed Virgin Mary; not because I believe this to be an uninteresting or peripheral question, but because to deal adequately with the complexities and confusions of feminist opinion here – ranging from the 'liberation Mariology' of Rosemary Radford Ruether to Mary Daly's representation of the Annunciation as a cosmic rape scene – in a book I have tried to make as short as possible, would have diverted attention from questions even more essential, and would have done little to correct the widespread and erroneous view that opposition to feminism within the Church has to do merely with the defence of a certain kind of old-fashioned 'obscurantist' churchmanship.

There are certain obvious dangers in writing such a book as this, one which concerns itself with describing and assessing an often bitterly militant movement and an overwhelmingly polemical literature. It is difficult, particularly when answering assaults on what have always been regarded as fundamental Christian truths to avoid adopting a tone equally trenchant. It is probably, indeed, sometimes necessary to do so: for here, if anywhere in modern theological discourse, is a controversy in which (to employ a suitably pugilistic metaphor) the gloves have been decisively removed. It is a controversy in which there can, in the end, be no neutral observers. For, as I hope to show, here we can see dramatically enacted (in a way capable of producing real changes in belief and practice) the underlying tension within modern western Christendom between, on the one hand, those who believe in a revealed religion, given once for all in God's own way, recorded in Holy Scripture, preserved and proclaimed through the ages in an unending series of languages and in ceaselessly varying cultural conditions by the Church his Body, always inexhaustibly relevant to man's changing needs and, on the other, a view which sees Christianity itself (and not merely its cultural expressions) as perpetually ephemeral, 'remade' for each new generation, relevant only when it mirrors the ever-shifting secular assumptions of the passing age.

Though the Christian feminist movement has established a debate in which a coolly dispassionate tone is not always easy, or even possible, to achieve, I have nevertheless attempted to avoid unnecessary offensiveness. Thus, I have avoided using the term 'priestess', except in quotation (even though after two years spent reading feminist theology its neo-pagan implications do not seem to me entirely out of place). The difficulties of language here are obvious enough: to use such terms as 'woman priest', 'sexist', 'consciousness-raising', 'women's movement' and the like, without quotation marks, implies an acceptance of the general view they are designed to promote. To use them invariably *inside* quotation marks can come to establish something like a hostile or even contemptuous tone which is not intended. Whether I have successfully avoided these extremes (and others) will be for others to say; and no doubt they will.

In the end, once the dust has finally settled over this controversy of the late twentieth century, it will be seen as not entirely fruitless only if it has succeeded in moving beyond mere polemic (however necessary in the short term) so as to stimulate a greater understanding of parts of the 'deposit of faith' hitherto taken too much for granted. The theological implications of feminism are wide-ranging, and I have not attempted here anything like a full or definitive rebuttal. One theme in particular has seemed to me specially crucial, however, a theme so deeply ingrained in the Christian tradition's awareness of God that until recently the idea that it should be considered merely as an optional 'metaphor' would have seemed devoid of sense: the theme of the Fatherhood of God and the Sonship of Christ, for Hoskyns and Davey 'the fundamental dogmas of primitive Christian theology and ethics'. Here, if anywhere, the feminist challenge will either concentrate the mind wonderfully, or fuddle it beyond recall. Why is it inappropriate (as undoubtedly most Christian people still instinctively feel it to be) to replace 'Abba! Father!' with 'God! Our Father and Mother'? Why should Christ have come into the world as God's Son, rather than as his daughter? There are, I believe, answers to these questions which have to do not with 'cultural relativity', but with profound religious truths to be perceived at a point where man's unaided reason is feeble and uncertain. I am under no illusion that I have succeeded in doing more here than to offer some tentative initial suggestions in an area which I hope will come under increasingly close scrutiny from theologians genuinely committed to elucidating for our times (and not simply replacing) the Church's historic faith.

My thanks are due to many, but especially to colleagues in Oxford who have helped me: to the Rev. Dr Jeffrey Steenson, for gathering liturgical and other material, both published and unpublished, in the United States; to Mr Henry Everett, for help with and translation of Hispanic material; to Dr Jonathan Webber of the Oxford University Centre for post-graduate Hebrew Studies and Dr Michael Argyle of the Department of Experimental Psychology for help on a number of questions within their general areas of competence; to the Rt Rev. Bishop Kallistos Ware, for a particularly helpful discussion on the theological problems approached in Part Three; to the Rev. Dr John Heidt, the Rev. Professor Wayne Hankey and Mr Charles Everitt for a number of suggestions and for countless conversations on topics germane to the problems examined in this book. My thanks are due to Fr Philip Ursell, the Principal of Pusey House for his endless support and patience, particularly as the time for the completion of the manuscript drew near, and to the mostly undergraduate congregation of Pusey House, where the breakfast conversation after daily Mass has been a never failing source of fresh insight. Above all, all my thanks are due to my wife, for more reasons than I can enumerate here: but above all for her unfailing sanity and humour, without which writing this book would have proved a greatly less pleasant task.

Solemnity of Mary, Mother of God, 1984
Pusey House,
Oxford

PART ONE

Beyond God the Father

Suppose the reformer stops saying that a good woman may be like God and begins saying that God is like a good woman. Suppose he says that we might just as well pray to 'Our Mother which art in Heaven' as to 'Our Father'. Suppose he suggests that the Incarnation might just as well have taken a female as a male form, and the Second Person of the Trinity be as well called the Daughter as the Son . . . .

Now it is surely the case that if all these supposals were ever carried into effect we should be embarked on a different religion. Goddesses have, of course, been worshipped: many religions have had priestesses. But they are religions quite different in character from Christianity.[1]

C. S. Lewis

The full moon is seen in the centre of the television screen. Clouds are moving slowly across it. A vague impression of awe is established by the sound of women's voices chanting: the sound is liturgical though unfamiliar - not unlike plainsong, but with something added, or rather perhaps something missing, so that the chanting induces a sense of indefinable unease. The camera moves to an altar of some kind. Between purple candles stands a female image. Calmly and authoritatively, a woman's voice explains:

> *Narrator*: It is the night of the full moon - a special time for women according to folk-lore. These women are worshipping their God, Inana. Inana is a female God.

The camera now shows a veiled priestess, leading the ritual for a small group of women in a suburban house in the north of England. The voice continues:

> *Narrator*: Rediscovering the Goddess tradition is one of the ways in which women are beginning to question the generally accepted view that God is Male.

The programme title appears on the screen: GOD THE MOTHER. Now, the priestess is shown explaining her religion, still 'veiled before strangers':

> *Priestess*: It is the mother who generates all things out of herself; it is the mother who nourishes, who gives milk; she is the primordial being, so to speak . . . if any human being is in God's image, it is the mother who, before any other, is in God's image. It is to the mother that we turn from the beginning of life and it is really in the mother that we see God.

The camera cuts back to the liturgy; the women seem to be chanting some form of creed.

There is an abrupt change of scene. We see a London townscape. The camera shows in the distance an image of patriarchy, the tower of the House of Lords; then it pans down on to a more recently constructed complex of buildings. The women's chanting has given way to the jaunty and un-mistakable sound of a school assembly. The hymn is 'Lord of the Dance'. The narrator continues:

> *Narrator*: The belief in a female Goddess is contrary to the teachings of Islam, Judaism and Christianity. This is a Church of England secondary school in London. From an early age, children are taught to pray to a Male God: God the Father.

Now, we are in a school assembly hall. A priest's voice makes itself heard: 'Let us now say together the prayer which our Saviour Christ himself taught us'. The camera lingers over one of the classic television code-images; here 'indoctrination' is conveyed by neat rows of children reciting in unison: 'Our Father, who art in heaven. . . .' The scene changes, and we see the children busily painting.

> *Narrator*: In their religious education class, the children are asked to illustrate their idea of God. Both boys and girls *all* depict God as a man.

Sure enough; there He is, in painting after painting; an old man with a beard, 'because he's been alive a long time' as one of the children puts it. As the screen now shows a more sophisticated rendering of this image, the calm voice sagely expounds:

> *Narrator*: The children's illustrations of a Male God are hardly surprising: they are carrying on a long tradition of religious art. In Western Culture, the image of a wise and caring father figure has always dominated the artistic imagination. The great painters have all seen God as a man. . . .[2]

The programme continues calmly on its way. The tone is reassuring; the technique familiar enough, that of a hundred other documentaries. There is a hint of controversy: 'women are beginning to question . . .'; but then, everyone is 'beginning to question'; that, in the world of the television documentary, is normality. What remain unquestioned are certain assumptions, which lie just beneath the surface, and which are quietly projected as though they were already ours. These assumptions are reinforced, not only by the way in which the programme is written, but in the use of certain techniques, infinitely more powerful once the small screen has begun to exert its mesmeric influence.

Chief among these is the 'voice-over': the calm and apparently omniscient tones of the unseen commentator, whose words will always carry more conviction than any which merely form the raw material being observed. Hence, when in the school assembly the priest is heard introducing the 'Our Father' as being 'the prayer which our saviour Christ himself taught us' (a not insignificant fact), the words have already been robbed of their authority: the priest, here, is a cultural phenomenon to be observed; only the voice-over is possessed of true knowledge. The children, we are to understand, see God as a 'wise and caring father-figure', not because to know him in this way is to be part of an authentic spiritual tradition, but because the understanding of God as 'Father' derives from an 'image' ingrained in something called 'western culture', and perpetuated by the indoctrination of children who, 'from an early age . . . are taught to pray to a Male God.' The most insistent underlying assumption of all is that religious beliefs can have no intrinsic authority of their own, but are projections from a dominant culture which has generated them for its own purposes.

Despite the programme's quiet, unhurried tone and carefully simulated atmosphere of objectivity, what we are witnessing is part of an attempted revolution in religious thought, which has been gathering momentum since the mid sixties, and which has an increasingly sure sense of its methods and objectives. The programme itself indicates the movement's growing confidence in handling the media of communication. Without alarming its Sunday evening audience unduly, the message is quietly but firmly pressed home: that there is now taking place a gradual, inevitable and desirable change. 'Women are beginning to question the generally accepted idea that God is Male'; 'The Male domination of religious language is something that religious leaders are coming to accept as a problem for women'; the voice-over's insistent message convincingly suggests the existence of a substantial and growing body of opinion.

Whether this opinion is soundly based is not discussed; it is enough that it exists. Few will have noticed that to call God our Father is *not* theologically equivalent to making the crude claim that 'God is Male'; few will have perceived the way in which tendentious ideas like 'the male domination of religious language' have been floated in for our unthinking acceptance. Meanwhile, on such questions as how *many* religious leaders are involved, or how many women as a proportion of other Christian women, the voice remains silent. It is necessary only to have prophesied; we live in the age of the self-fulfilling prophecy. And certainly, if enough 'religious leaders' can be convinced that there is a real issue here (no one should underestimate the appetite of western religious leaders for 'real issues'), the job will be half-done: in the end, there are few siren calls more seductive than the invitation to a sense of grievance (justified or not) when it carries with it the heady excitement of being part of a righteous cause.

1

Feminist Consciousness

The sense of grievance which underlies the assumptions of the 'Women's Movement', both inside and outside the Church, becomes in the end one of the most fascinating and enigmatic characteristics of feminist utterance. It is not so much that the resentment *exists* (though it can be of a virulence quite startling to men and women unfamiliar with hard-core feminist literature). It is rather that feeling aggrieved appears to be itself a necessary primary objective. It is a state of mind, almost a spiritual condition, which seems at times not so much a natural reaction to perceived injustice as itself a means of perception, a kind of lens through which familiar landmarks can take on horrid and undreamed-of shapes. 'How', asks Paula Fredriksen Landes, 'could feminist consciousness have developed without anger?':

Anger growing with the realization of the psychological and cultural manipulation of women; anger at the tremendous power men have had over women's lives to induce feelings of dependence and powerlessness, discouraging growth, independence and individuation; anger at those religions which claim to provide moral guidance and liberation, but instead amplify this sexist oppression. Women turning to these religions find heaven a male domain, God and Jesus male deities, and theology built upon and presupposing the experience of male theologians. Women's experience is denied, not even recognized in this religious cosmos. For those feminists concerned with the religious dimension of life, the absence of any spiritual tradition which resonates with their experience and which grounds women in a religious cosmos is one of the most insidious aspects of western culture. To submit to the guidance of traditional religion is to become vulnerable to a kind of spiritual rape . . .[3]

The great difficulty for most people (including the overwhelming majority of women) on reading such a passage has less to do with the question of whether or not its analysis can be sustained, than with the problem of discovering what it is that can have prompted anyone to write it in the first place. It is possible, for instance, strongly to disagree with the political and theological analysis of a Latin-American liberation theologian, while sharing his perception of the very serious social conditions to which his theology is for him the inevitable reaction. But the 'injustice' under which women suffer in the Christian tradition is not merely ignored by Christian men, but entirely imperceptible to most Christian women too. Their reaction to such a passage (delivered with varying degrees of irritation) is liable to be, quite simply, 'what on earth is the woman *talking* about?'

Many feminists, of course, are quite well aware of this. They simply see it as further evidence for their claim that women have been degraded to the point where they are no longer able to see how degraded they are. Not that this ignorance brings immunity from feminist invective. 'If you are an average female reader of this book', wrote Arianna Stassinopoulos in her antifeminist polemic *The Female Woman* (1973), 'you are seen by the leaders of Women's Lib as perverse, servile, dishonest, inefficient, inconsistent, idiotic, passive, ignorant, and in-effectual' (all adjectives culled from a selection of current feminist writings). 'The moral excuse for this display of contempt and derision', she continues, 'is that women are not responsible for their condition; Women's Libbers can safely revile all other women by portraying them as the victims of a male dominated society.'[4] The radical feminist claims, in fact to be possessed of a means of understanding reality denied to other women. She is the recipient of a special knowledge; her 'feminist consciousness' is a sort of *gnosis*, enabling her for the first time in human history to give a true account of the relations of men and women through the ages. Now, she can declare with Mary Daly that 'the Female Self is the Enemy targeted by the State of War'; she can join battle in the conviction that 'this self becomes ultimately threatening when she bonds in networks with other Self-accepting Female Selves.'[5]

The immediate political context for 'the new consciousness among women' which led to the mushroom growth during the early seventies of 'women's liberation' was, suggests Sheila Rowbotham, 'the inchoate radicalism of the student left in the late sixties and the specifically female contradictions con-fronted by women who entered higher education.'[6] This needs some qualifications; the American pioneers of the new feminism had been active since the early sixties, and their activities were more widely based. But certainly, in both Europe and America, there was for some women a consciousness that - together with a whole generation - they were at odds with all existing institutions; and this together with a feeling of isolation even from the radical generation itself undoubtedly led some women to see themselves as being in a special way alienated from their culture and driven to make a new sub-culture for themselves. This feeling was by no means always unjustified by the behaviour of radical men: to the question of how he saw the position of women in the Student Non-violent Coordinating Committee (SNCC) Stokely Carmichael, in a one-word answer that has passed into the folklore of the women's movement, answered simply 'prone'.[7] And this feeling of double alienation appears to have generated - or at least to have been accompanied by - what can only be described as a distinct tendency to paranoia, a tendency which was to become, in one way or another, a characteristic feature of the radical feminist consciousness.

An interesting case history is that of Carol P. Christ and Judith Plaskow, whose collaboration in feminist theology began in the autumn of 1969, when they were both graduate students in theology at Yale University. After the inaugural meeting of the first feminist group at Yale, they retired to a local 'hangout', to discover that they shared many frustrations over the Yale graduate syllabus in theology. They disliked the programme of studies, which they thought should not be exclusively Christian in its content; and both thought that theology ought to be more concerned with such issues as starvation in Biafra and the Vietnamese War. Their discontent was not confined to academic and political issues: 'we both felt that the male faculty and students saw us primarily as women, not as theologians.'

Their embattled solidarity grew over the next two years, as they called on each other to 'verify our sanity and intelligence and to seek support in specific situations':

> 'I said so and so about Tillich in a seminar today', one of us would say, 'and everyone ignored me. Was I wrong, or am I stupid?' 'No. You aren't stupid. That's an important point', the other would reply. 'They didn't hear you because you're a woman.'[8]

It is surely not entirely insensitive to comment that those without the special handicap of belief in a conspiracy are better able to adjust to the rough and tumble of academic life, in which great discoveries (real or apparent) may be ignored or deflated, in which teachers and fellow students are less convinced than perhaps they might be of the universal importance of one's own special interests, and in which tutors and supervisors are likely to be firm, even brusque, when they see an *idée fixe* dominating a student's mind so as to unbalance his or her understanding of a whole subject. It is difficult not to have a certain sympathy for the teachers of these two determined young women:

We remember the day we proposed to a professor that we might take one of our comprehensives on the history of Christian attitudes towards women. Although we were armed with seven or eight pages of sources on the subject, we had no sooner mentioned the topic when he slammed his fist on the table and shouted, 'Not for me, you're not!' We also remember Carol's turning in a seminar paper on Barth's view of women to a professor who glanced at the title and remarked that he had never considered *that* a very important topic. He then went on to discuss the papers presented by the males in the class.[9]

They go on to comment that

it is little wonder that, given repeated incidents like this, we might neither of us have finished graduate school at all without the support, encouragement, and intellectual comradeship we gave each other. . . . Yale made us feminists . . . and Yale made us confront the male bias of theology in which the sexist attitudes of our colleagues were rooted.

Like the wider secular movement of which it is part, the Christian Feminist Movement is small in numbers, though like the wider Women's Movement, it has certainly made significant advances during the seventies and early eighties. In the early seventies, Christ and Plaskow were organizing women theology students in such events as the 'liberation' of the only lavatory (for men) in the stacks of the Yale Divinity School Library; by the end of the decade both were teaching University courses on 'women and religion' with the help of a growing literature, including Rosemary Radford Ruether's collection of essays *Religion and Sexism* (1974), and Elizabeth Clark's and Herbert Richardson's *Women and Religion* (1977).[10]

The Christian feminist movement is still a largely middle class one, and in this, too, it mirrors faithfully the 'women's movement' as a whole which, despite some activity in the Trade Union movement, remains as Arianna Stassinopoulos cuttingly described it in 1973, 'not a people's movement . . . [but] an eclectic sect drawn from the trendier section of the middle classes'.[11] What *has* developed, in some ways dramatically, is the movement's effectiveness. In 1970, it was still possible for

Germaine Greer, writing in England, to note that '...
Women's Liberation Workshops are appearing in the suburban
haunts of the educated housewife, and in the universities.
There is no great coherence in their theory and no particular
imagination or efficiency to be observed in their methods.'[12] By
1978, David Bouchier could observe, surveying the radical new
left movements of the late sixties, that though most of them
had made little impact on the lives and consciousness of most
people, the feminist movement, by contrast, 'in an astonishingly
short space of time, created an almost universal awareness of
women's problems and demands in western Europe and the
United States, together with substantial changes in social
policy.'[13]

2
Revolution and Nothing Less

What is important to note is that the Women's Movement will
not be assuaged by any such reforms; it is not a reformist
movement but a revolutionary one. The radical feminist fights
the battle of the sexes in deadly earnest. She profoundly
believes that she lives in a culture which for millennia has been
expressly fashioned for her degradation. The aim, no matter
how ill-defined, is revolution and nothing less, a revolution
involving more than a mere assertion of women's rights. In
Kate Millett's words,

> As the largest alienated element in our society, and because of their
> numbers, passion, and length of oppression, its largest revolution-
> ary base, women might come to play a leadership part in social
> revolution, quite unknown before in history.[14]

It is clear that for the Christian women's movement it is secular
feminism which provides the initial impetus and, to some
extent, the ideological nurture for its own revolutionary
objective: the substantial reconstruction of the Christian
religion itself. The year after Kate Millett's *Sexual Politics*

(1970) 'rocketed her', in Mary Daly's words, 'into the role of American counterpart to Simone de Beauvoir',[15] Daly was writing (in an essay significantly entitled 'after the death of God the Father') that

> As the women's revolution begins to have its effect upon the fabric of society, transforming it from patriarchy into something that never existed before - into a diarchal situation that is radically new - it will, I believe, become the greatest potential challenge to Christianity to rid itself of its oppressive tendencies or go out of business. Beliefs and values that have held sway for thousands of years will be questioned as never before.[16]

And the process of doctrinal reconstruction is to be applied not to accretions or to distortions of fundamental Christian beliefs but at the heart of the biblical revelation itself. Chief among the beliefs and 'oppressive tendencies' to be dealt with is the 'image of the Father God, spawned in the human imagination, and sustained as plausible by patriarchy'; it is to be swept away as the Women's Revolution changes 'our whole vision of reality'.[17] 'Since "God" is Male, the male is God', Daly asserts elsewhere; 'God the Father legitimates all earthly God-fathers.' It takes no great effort of imagination to predict that she will go on to assert that 'the idea of a unique divine incarnation in a male, the God man of the "hypostatic union" is inherently sexist and oppressive. Christolatry is idolatry.'[18]

It is safe to say that such a view will not overnight become generally accepted by Christian men and women. Nevertheless, it forms a vital part of the ideological background to a controversy which has already had a profound effect within the Anglican communion, and which, it can be confidently predicted, will increasingly perplex Roman Catholics, particularly in countries like Holland and the United States: the question of the ordination of women to the priesthood within the historic threefold ministry of bishop, priest and deacon. These last two passages by Mary Daly (a formerly Roman Catholic theologian, who now describes herself as 'post-Christian', but who continues to be a university teacher of theology and to exert a considerable influence on feminists within the Church) are, indeed, quoted by Elisabeth Schüssler

Fiorenza, then a teacher of 'women's courses in theology' at a
Catholic university, as part of a general case for the ordination
of women to the priesthood. Of Daly's contention that the
doctrine of the incarnation is 'inherently sexist and oppressive',
she comments simply that 'The assertion of some theologians
that Christ was male and, therefore that women cannot be
ordained as priests and represent Christ before the community
appears to substantiate Dr Daly's contention'[19] (my italics).
Fiorenza's inference here is not, it should be noted, that some
theologians have wrongly *understood* the implications of the
incarnation, but that the doctrine itself is false. To worship
Christ as God is 'Christolatry'; and one clear purpose of
ordaining women to the priesthood, perhaps the overriding
purpose, is to achieve some movement in theological understanding. 'If women were admitted to the full leadership in
Church and theology', Fiorenza asserts (referring to the
priesthood), 'the need would no longer exist to affirm
theologically the maleness of God and Christ and to suppress
the Spirit who moves women to full participation in the
Christian Church and ministry.'[20]

Having noted in passing a now familiar device, the polemic
trivialization of the issue in such formulae as 'the maleness of
God and Christ', it is important at this stage to observe that
there is no question here of any simple readjustment or merely
reformist advance for 'women's rights'. Nor, in the end, have
Christian feminists any but a short-term tactical interest in
'participation in the Christian Church and ministry' as they
have been inherited from previous ages. As Susan Dowell and
Linda Hurcombe suggest, 'female priesthood is peripheral
unless it revolutionizes the system'.[21] The long-term feminist
strategy is no secret to those who actually go to the trouble of
reading the literature intended for internal consumption by the
Christian feminist movement, though it is often explained
quite differently for a wider audience. In England, for instance,
as Sara Maitland explains,

> seeking to be persuasive and attractive to likely Synodical voters,
> MOW [the Movement for the Ordination of women] is often
> markedly conservative in its approaches. Its national committee

includes a bishop and several priests and its projected image of ordained women is determinedly unthreatening, and uncritical of existing structures.[22]

We may certainly observe a tendency (not untypical of radical communities bent on advance through reformist attrition) to express policy differently for different audiences; sometimes there will be a perceptible shift from the revolutionary to the reformist style within the same pronouncement. Radical objectives are, as it were, encoded, so that they may be persuasive to the average well-meaning liberal; who likes to flirt with danger without committing himself too far to any truly radical change, and whose support is vital for any advance.

One way of making such objectives 'safe' for public consumption would be to describe them in the language of political rather than theological radicalism (since left-wing theologians have a reputation for asserting an orthodox understanding of incarnational teaching). Hence, in the television series already quoted, the 'voice-over' is heard to feed in a question as to whether English campaigners understand the *political* consequences of women's ordination to the priesthood, to be answered by Deaconess Una Kroll, perhaps the English movement's best known spokesman:

> *Kroll*: Yes, of course I do, and that's what's so frightening to everybody; everyone knows that that's exactly what I do want to see. An overturning of the hierarchical system, a coming of a much more consensus system and a much more holistic attitude towards men and women and in the way in which the laity participate in the Church. Yes, it would change, it would humanize the Church, the structures of the Church.[23]

What precisely this means is not immediately apparent, but we may reasonably look to the general context of Deaconess Kroll's views for clarification in the original feminist idiom, perhaps in some such words as these by Elisabeth Fiorenza:

> Only if we, women and men, are able to live in nonsexist Christian communities, to celebrate nonsexist Christian liturgies, and to think in nonsexist theological terms and imagery will we be able to formulate a genuine Christian feminist spirituality.[24]

This in itself is little more explicit. But it is clear that, at the very least, it means not only that our whole heritage of Church and ministry is to undergo radical reconstruction: so too is the understanding of the nature of God that has sustained it. Rosemary Radford Ruether, perhaps the most influential feminist theologian still within the Church, puts it succinctly enough: 'the conservatives', she admits, 'are correct in recognizing that the revolution represented by the ordination of women threatens the whole symbolic structure.'[25]

This last phrase, 'the whole symbolic structure', indicates a vital dimension in the debate, perception of which (as against the lack of any such perception) tends to distinguish two broad groupings: orthodox defenders of Judaeo-Christian tradition together with radical feminists on the one hand and, on the other, establishment liberals who have espoused the feminist cause, together with what might be termed 'revisionist' feminists. The two groups are interestingly paralleled in contemporary Judaism: the 'revisionists' are those who, in the words of the feminist psychologist of religion Naomi Goldenberg 'do not see . . . reforms as challenging the basic nature of Christianity and Judaism. Instead, they understand themselves to be improving the practice of their religions by encouraging women to share the responsibility of worship equally with men'.[26] Goldenberg, very much a radical, disagrees in terms which would be accepted by any 'conservative' (indeed, she goes on to praise Pope Paul VI's argument against women's ordination to the priesthood for its 'impressive knowledge of how image and symbol operate in the human mind'). 'The reforms which Christian and Jewish women are proposing', she uncompromisingly asserts, 'are major departures from tradition. . . . The nature of a religion lies in the nature of the symbols it exalts in ritual and doctrine.'[27] Though a Christian believer would find it necessary to qualify this (for instance by saying that the nature of a religion can be *perceived* in the nature of its symbols) Goldenberg here can be seen to introduce an essential level of discussion nearly always avoided by those who - at least in public - claim that a change such as the ordination of women to the priesthood constitutes a merely reformist adjustment to the existing ministry of the Church.

15

3

The Dark Spaces Beyond

Goldenberg's own position has an obvious fascination for feminist theologians still within the Church and straining every nerve-ending to rewrite Christian tradition to accommodate their 'feminist consciousness'. Here, her general argument is respectfully summarized (and somewhat bowdlerized to make it acceptable for publication in *Concilium*, a respectable liberal Catholic publication), by Catharina Halkes, a member of the theology faculty of the Catholic University of Nijmegen with special responsibility for teaching related to 'religion and feminism':

> . . . if women rise up and assume the place that they should legitimately have in society, that society will change and take on a different aspect. But, she asks, what will happen to God if women in many churches demand the places that they should have in the structures of those churches, after having acquired clarity through their feminist criticism of religion? What will take place, she argues, is a 'changing of the Gods'. This will happen because women will transform religion, expose its roots, and eradicate the image of God the Father that oppresses them. She too speaks of a 'core-symbolism' that is one-sidedly male and points to an interaction between Father and Son that marginalizes women.[28]

It is clear enough that we have here arrived at (and in the case of some feminist theologians passed through) the farthest limits separating Christian belief and a kind of apostasy, though one which has no vestige of the common Victorian complaint, 'loss of faith'. Christian feminist theologians who inhabit this remote altitude, where the air of traditional Christian belief is thin but still breathable and where they can also look beyond to the dark mysterious spaces that beckon, are not irreligious. They are, almost, too religious; they have reached a point where being religious, having the religious dimension available on their terms, is more important than anything else. It is almost as though God has ceased to be for them an independently existent being, in a living relationship with whom their spiritual lives unfold, and who has revealed himself to the human race in his own way. The idea of revelation, indeed (as we shall see), is part of a whole complex of potentially 'authoritarian' and 'sexist' doctrines which feminist theologians regard with deep suspicion. God, in this understanding, becomes an extension of human self-perception rather than a source of growth beyond the self, a growth which will always, in an authentically Christian spirituality, involve surrender; the seed dying in the earth before it can grow and multiply. It is precisely here, indeed, that feminist spirituality recoils, seeing in such surrender a trap for women; and feminist theologians who have finally made the break with their spiritual past are those who can now, unrestrained by the fetters still weakly restraining their Christian sisters, assert the autonomous human self (in their case the female self) as the true source of religious energy and power.

So it is, that Professor Carol P. Christ could stand, in the spring of 1978, before a conference on the theme 'The Great Goddess re-emerging' at the University of California, to open her keynote address by referring to a Broadway play, at the end of which:

> A tall beautiful black woman rises from despair to cry out, 'I found God in myself and I loved her fiercely'. Her discovery is echoed by women around the country who meet spontaneously in small groups on full moons, solstices, and equinoxes to celebrate the Goddess as symbol of life and death powers and waxing and waning energies in the universe and in themselves.[29]

Any doubt as to what this means is removed by Professor Christ, in a passage (here quoted more fully) from the feminist writer and witch, 'Starhawk':

> It is the night of the full moon. Nine women stand in a circle, on a rocky hill above the city. The western sky is rosy with the setting sun; in the east the moon's face begins to peer above the horizon. Below, electric lights wink on the ground like fallen Stars. A young woman raises a steel knife and cries out, a wail echoed by the others as they begin the dance. They circle wildly around a cauldron of smoldering herbs, feeling the power rising within them until they unite in ecstasy. The priestess cries again, and all drop to the earth,

17

exhausted, but filled with an overwhelming sense of peace. The woman pours out a cup of wine onto the earth, refills it and raises it high. 'Hail, Tana, Mother of mothers!' she cries. 'Awaken from your long sleep, and return to your children again!'[30]

Of what interest to Christians are such lurid glimpses into contemporary 'post-Christian' religious belief and practice? The kind of religious activity proposed by Professor Christ as a real option for women today seems unlikely to provide a model for women within the Church, however radical. Nor is the theology of the 'goddess movement' explicitly accepted by Christian feminist theologians, and the best known of them, Rosemary Ruether, has expressed strong reservations about it. A theologian like Mary Daly, furthermore, is now so wild in her assertions about the Christian tradition that we would naturally expect such influence as she once had on Christian feminists (and through them on their establishment liberal supporters) to have largely dissipated. Here, for example, is her 'post-Christian' mutation from the doctrine of the second coming of Christ:

> I suggest that the mechanism of reversal has been at the root of the idea that the 'Antichrist' must be something 'evil'. What if this is not the case at all? What if the idea has arisen out of the male's unconscious dread that women will rise up and assert the power robbed from us? . . . The Antichrist dreaded by the Patriarchs may be the surge of consciousness, the spiritual awakening, that can bring us beyond Christolatry into a fuller stage of conscious participation in the *living* God.
>
> Seen from this perspective the Antichrist and the Second Coming of Women are synonymous. This Second Coming is not a return of Christ but a new arrival of female presence, once strong and powerful, but enchained since the dawn of patriarchy . . .
>
> The Second Coming, then, means that the prophetic dimension in the symbol of the great Goddess . . . is the key to salvation from servitude to structures that obstruct human becoming . . .[31]

Nevertheless, whatever the disagreements on theological issues we ought in fairness to assume, what seems more striking is the extent of the agreement which remains between Christian and post-Christian feminists. The wildest and most spiritually dangerous beliefs are not enough to break the solidarity of 'sisterhood': and though the extract from Mary Daly which I have just quoted is by no means the most immoderate or the most anti-Christian that could have been found in the book from which it is taken (*Beyond God the Father: towards a philosophy of women's liberation*), it remains immovably on Christian feminist lists of recommended reading. Susan Dowell, for instance, has no hesitation (after almost wistfully referring to non-Christian 'groups . . . engaged in the creation of an entirely new spiritual consciousness, ecological and woman-affirming') in admitting that 'contemporary feminist theology owes a great deal to Mary Daly and her book *Beyond God the Father*'.[32] The conclusion becomes more and more irresistible, the more the evidence is surveyed: 'feminist consciousness' is the channel for the primary revelation, by which all others are to be judged.

There can be little doubt that the neo-pagan 'ecological and woman-affirming' spiritual consciousness to which Dowell refers has a more than passing interest for some Christian feminists. As Dowell rightly asserts, it is a mistake to suppose that 'when attachment to . . . religious institutions dies, then spiritual longing and quest fade away',[33] and the combination of spiritual longing with disaffection from existing beliefs and structures, together with an emphasis (sometimes under Jungian influence) on myth and ritual, has led many women to an interest in liturgical experimentation, sometimes drawing heavily for inspiration on what Halkes euphemistically calls 'comparative religion'.[34] The following outline for a feminist ritual is one of a number produced by a 'workshop' of around thirty-five women from all over the United States, which met in 1978:

GREETING
(The gathered group exchanges words and signs of peace)
INVOKING THE POWER OF THE GODDESS
PRAYER OF CONFESSION
(A unison prayer expressing ways we participate in our own oppression by not claiming the power of being)

COMMUNAL STATEMENT OF ACCEPTANCE AND PARDON
SILENCE

Then, the poem 'For the unknown Goddess', by Elizabeth Brewster, is read:

> Lady, the unknown goddess,
> we have prayed long enough only
> To Yahweh the thunder god.
>
> Now we should pray to you again
> goddess of a thousand names and faces
> Ceres Venus Demeter Isis
> Ianna Queen of Heaven
> or by whatever name
> you would be known

The 'ecological' dimension of the poem is important: 'present-day ecological concerns', as one of the women involved in the workshop puts it elsewhere, 'are in some sense a renewal of the awareness of the earth and the profound linkages of life-processes within the cosmos'. Thus, the poem continues:

> you who sprang from the sea
> you who are present in the moisture of love
> who live in the humming cells
> of all life . . .
> and you who are earth
> you with your beautiful ruined face
> wrinkled by all
> that your children have done to you . . .
>
> we invoke your name
> which we no longer know
>
> and pray to you
> to restore our humanity
> as we restore your divinity.

The order of service now continues:

A RITUAL RESPONSE
(*Lying on the floor to listen to the humming in our cells; a walk outside to become aware of the earth; a meditation, repeating phrases, noting emotions evoked by the poem, etc.*)

AN INTERPRETATION OF THE POEM AND TESTIFYING ABOUT
EXPERIENCES OF BEING AND NONBEING

SILENCE

PRAYERS
(For ourselves
For people who help us claim the power of being
For the strengthening of our faith
For the power to create being in other people)

BLESSING RITUAL
(The women turn to one another and ask for words and signs of
blessing. This may be done individually or collectively, such as in
the laying on of hands.)[35]

The liturgy has all the marks of a certain kind of post-
Christian feminist spirituality: the firm rejection of the Judaeo-
Christian monotheist tradition (with more than a hint of
nostalgia for the *status quo ante*); the Feuerbachian and
Marxist notion that, in Marx's words, '*Man makes religion*',
that 'religion is the self-consciousness and self-feeling of man'
(though without the logical conclusion of this assertion, that
'the abolition of religion as the *illusory* happiness of the people
is required for their *real* happiness');[36] the determination which
results from this, to throw off allegiance to a 'Male God', and to
remake the divine in the image of woman; the accompanying
assertion of the female will, in Carol Christ's words 'the
positive valuation of will in a Goddess centered ritual';[37] it is all
here.

And yet, this rite was not composed primarily for women
who have moved beyond the structures of the Christian
Church: it is published in a book which aims to create
'materials for prayer, meditation and worship drawn from
women's experiences of the holy to provide ways *to enrich the*
Christian tradition . . .'[38] This material is offered, by women of
impeccable 'establishment' credentials, as 'an excellent resource
for any congregation wishing to undertake the difficult task of
changing the image of God in its liturgy.'[39]

It is, of course, difficult to say how widely within the Church
such ritual material is actually used; much of it seems to be for
small exclusive groups of women meeting in private houses,

and is unlikely to involve large numbers. Certainly, the rite we have just examined is unlikely to catch on for regular use in any congregation, even in one which has decided 'to undertake the difficult task of changing the image of God in its liturgy'.

4
Why Worry?

The question, then, remains: of what interest to most Christian people are the religious beliefs and practices of some radical feminists, even of Christian feminists? If it is true that some of them are strongly attracted towards a non-Christian (or even anti-Christian) 'spiritual consciousness', will not this very fact tend to neutralize their influence on Christians more deeply committed to the existing structures of the Church and to the development and renewal of the Christian tradition they have received? Will it not even insulate them from the liberal reformists on whom they are politically dependent for progress towards the changes they seek? As a senior Jesuit said to the author, 'does this kind of theology really have a future?'

The answer must be that it already has a present. Just as there are wide open lines of communication between feminists within the Church and post-Christian feminists decidedly outside it, with few discernible doctrinal inhibitions or overriding biblical loyalties to anchor Christian feminists clearly within their own tradition, so too, within the Church, there is clear evidence of a more than respectful attitude towards radical Christian feminists among influential liberal theologians. In posing the question 'as to whether God is our Father', in an edition of *Concilium* devoted to the matter, the Editors Edward Schillebeeckx and Johannes Baptist Metz are partly, as they admit (and probably primarily) 'following the lead of feminist theology';[40] and in her own contribution 'The Themes of Protest in Feminist Theology against God the Father',[41] Fr Schillebeeckx's colleague Catharina Halkes quite seriously examines four major feminist theologians (apparently as representative), of whom three are in different ways devotees of the 'goddess movement' (in one case at least in the form of feminist witchcraft), and only one, Rosemary Radford Ruether, actually within the Church and in any way critical of the movement's fiercely anti-Christian stance.[42] The grounds of Ruether's objections are themselves not wholly reassuring, and as we shall see have since been modified.

The Catholic University teacher Halkes expresses herself as being able 'at least at present' (*sic*) to 'go along with' Ruether's opposition to the movement, though she thinks that 'Carol Christ's answer, that the prophetic tradition in the Bible . . . has not *in any sense* been of benefit to women, calls for very serious consideration'.[43] It is worth noting that in her own contribution to the same issue of *Concilium*, 'The female nature of God: a problem in contemporary religious life', Ruether has shown herself more sympathetic to the goddess movement, asserting that

> . . . it is possible that we are witnessing in this movement the first stirrings of what may become a new stage of human religious consciousness. This possibility cannot be ruled out by the critical Christian. It may be that we have allowed divine revelation through the prophets and through Jesus to be so corrupted by an idolatrous androcentrism, that a fuller understanding of God that truly includes the female as person must come as superseding and judging patriarchal religion.[44]

The flaws in this bizarre movement are now seen by Professor Ruether not as fatal disqualifications, but as 'immaturities', to be outgrown as humanity moves towards a new stage of development in which 'God(ess) must be seen as beyond both maleness and femaleness', and in which, encompassing the full humanity of both men and women, 'God(ess) also speaks as . . . redeemer from the stereotyped roles in which men as "masculine" and women as "feminine" have been cast in patriarchal society.'[45]

There can be little doubt that the women's movement, both in its Christian and post-Christian religious manifestations, and in its unadulteratedly secularist (and more generally influential) form, has not been without effect on the thinking of some key modern churchmen. The influence of the secular movement has been in some ways more immediately apparent, and there are obvious reasons why this should be so. Thus, the Rt Rev. Kenneth Woollcombe, then Bishop of Oxford, speaking in the Church of England's General Synod Debate on the motion 'there are no fundamental objections to the ordination of women to the priesthood', urged the acceptability of developments in the Church's doctrine of God, but (perhaps deliberately) did so in a way which left unclear the relevance of this question to that of the ordination of women. Bishop Woolcombe preferred to engage the question of priestly ordination least obscurely not on theological ground, but on the battleground opened up at this time by the proponents of secular 'equal opportunities' legislation: though denying that the Church was 'responding to sociological pressure', he asked the Synod to accept the principle that 'if the world is making up its own mind at the same time, then it is right that we should think together',[46] clearly indicating his view that the priesthood should be seen in this context in the same way as any other career.

Certainly, some liberal Anglican bishops have not been slow to perceive the opportunities presented by the modern feminist movement. The Rt Rev. Paul Moore, Bishop of New York, a veteran of the women's ordination campaign in the United States, as well as of other campaigns of the radical sixties, first became aware of 'women's issues', when his wife introduced him to Simone de Beauvoir's *The Second Sex*, long before there was a visible movement.[47] Gradually, 'as the talk about it increased and the literature proliferated', he and other Episcopalian bishops became increasingly involved: in the mid-sixties, James A. Pike, Bishop of California, caused the first debate on the women's movement in the House of Bishops. In 1970 the issue of women's ordination to the priesthood came before the American Church's general convention, and 'when permission to ordain women priests was defeated a second time in 1973', as Bishop Moore recalls, 'the women's movement within the Church was going strong'.[48]

It would be unfair, however to suggest that 'liberals' in the American Episcopal Church were responding entirely to secular ideological influences, though the dates of the various debates just referred to seem to indicate a remarkably swift and sensitive response to the new wave of American radical feminist activity. But Bishop Moore, for instance, indicates also the theological dimension in his support for this new cause. Thus, he believes that 'the average Christian or Jew images God as masculine and responds psychologically to God as a father', not because God has revealed himself in this way, but as the result of a 'projection of human qualities upon God . . .'.[49] Bishop Moore's conclusion is equally familiar:

> If God is Male, not female, then men are intrinsically better than women. It follows then, that until the emphasis on maleness in the image of God is redressed, the women of the world cannot be entirely liberated. For if God is thought of as simply and exclusively male, then the very cosmos seems sexist.[50]

And the purpose of ordaining women is not only the reformist one of allowing them to 'take their rightful place in the Church':

> God as Father and God as Son invoked by a male minister during worship creates in the unconscious, the intuitive, the emotive part of your belief an unmistakable male God. However, when women begin to read the Scripture, when they preside at the Eucharist, when they wear the symbolic robes of Christ, this unconscious perception will begin to be redressed and the femininity of God will begin to be felt.[51]

Though less crisply expressed, the roots of this thinking in the work not only of radical Christian feminist writers such as Rosemary Ruether, but also of clearly anti-Christian theologians like Mary Daly (cf. for instance Daly's 'if God is Male, the Male is God'), seems to be fairly clear: at the very least we are entitled to say that there are suggestive affinities.

But again, the question poses itself: should more or less orthodox Christians really be worried by this kind of speculation? In particular, should not Anglicans, who have often held up tolerance above many other virtues, be patient in this matter too? Why should we not once again say, in the words of Gamaliel's defence of the Apostles, 'refrain from these men and let them alone: for if this counsel or this work be of men it will fail; if it be of God, you cannot stand against it'?

The answer, however reluctant we may be to give it, must be that in this case to follow Gamaliel's principle would be to allow ourselves a luxury unwarranted in the Church's present condition; for in the time it could take for the truth to assert itself (possibly a matter of decades) profound and lasting damage to the Church could well be caused, and probably has been caused in some provinces of the Anglican communion. For here, we are not considering an intellectual fashion, which can pass as though it had never been. Like other revolutionary ideologies, this one aims at perpetuating itself in institutional changes difficult, perhaps even impossible, to reverse. Women's ordination, as we have repeatedly seen, is thought of by many of those most committed to achieving it as a means of installing immovably, in the permanent structures of the Church itself, a fundamental shift in the Christian tradition: to ordain women as priests will be to change at its foundations our idea of God. And this is no intemperate and unfounded accusation but, as I have shown, an ambition coolly announced by the most substantial feminist writers. It may be that this ambition should be achieved; but it is right that Christian people should at least know what many of those who are seeking to bring about the change really intend.

For it is important clearly to understand that the Fatherhood of God is not the only Christian doctrine feminist writers have in their sights, as will partly emerge from time to time as the book proceeds. But it is the first, in a whole series of theological dominoes; once it has fallen, other allegedly 'sexist' Christian ideas will follow, and are already under baleful scrutiny. The incarnation of Christ and the doctrine of the Trinity; sin and the fall of man; the doctrine of grace; the very notion of revelation and of the authority of the Bible as the inspired word of God: the feminist theologians who have most effectively fuelled this controversy are bent on the undermining of all these great supporting arches of the Church's tradition. It is difficult to see how, in the words of Naomi Goldenberg, 'Christianity can survive the very basic changes that will have to be made' in adapting it to the feminist vision. 'There will of course', she goes on to say, 'be nothing to prevent people who practise new religions from calling themselves Christians. . . . Undoubtedly, many followers of new faiths will still cling to old labels. But a merely semantic veneer of tradition ought not to hide the fact that very nontraditional faiths will be practised.'[52]

In the end, what is, surely, at stake in the whole feminist theological enterprise is whether or not we are prepared to receive God's revelation of himself; whether, indeed there can be any such revelation. For, in C. S. Lewis's words,

> . . . Christians think that God Himself has taught us how to speak of Him. To say that it does not matter is to say that all the masculine imagery is not inspired, is merely human in origin, or else that, though inspired, it is quite arbitrary and unessential. And this is surely intolerable: or, if tolerable, it is an argument not in favour of Christian priestesses but against Christianity.[53]

And the Church's understanding of the masculine and feminine principles in creation, and of the roles fulfilled by men and women in the Christian tradition, are not our own to adjust at our whim:

> . . . for there we are dealing with male and female not merely as facts of nature but as the live and awful shadows of realities utterly beyond our control and largely beyond our direct knowledge. Or rather, we are not dealing with them but (as we shall soon learn if we meddle) they are dealing with us.[54]

Lewis was writing in the late nineteen-forties: nearly forty years on, his words have a chilling and increasingly unmistakable ring of prophetic truth. Whether, for the Anglican communion at least, the sound will be heard by generations to come as a warning note or as a funeral knell may depend on future events as yet only half guessed at.

NOTES TO PART ONE

1   C. S. Lewis, 'Priestesses in the Church?', from *God in the Dock* (London 1979), p. 90: originally published in *Time and Tide* XXIX (14 Aug 1948), pp. 830-1.

2 'God the Mother', the third 'Credo' programme in a series of three under the general title *Behind the Veil;* London Weekend Television, 14 March 1982.

3 Paula Fredriksen Landes, book review, *Signs* VI(2), Winter 1980, pp. 328-9.

4 Arianna Stassinopoulos, *The Female Women* (London 1973), p. 13.

5 Mary Daly, *Gyn/Ecology* (London 1979), p. 379.

6 Sheila Rowbotham, *Woman's Consciousness, Man's World* (London 1973), p. ix.

7 See, for instance, Anna Coote and Beatrix Campbell, *Sweet Freedom* (London 1982), p. 13; Coote and Campbell comment (p. 14) that 'Judging by the number of times that remark has been quoted since, it did as much to fuel the fire for a women's movement as the publication of *The Feminine Mystique.*'

8 Carol P. Christ and Judith Plaskow (eds.), *Womanspirit Rising: A Feminist Reader in Religion* (New York 1979), p. ix.

9 ibid., pp. ix-x.

10 ibid., p. xi.

11 Stassinopoulos, op. cit., p. 142.

12 Germaine Greer, *The Female Eunuch* (London 1970), p. 300.

13 David Bouchier, *Idealism and Revolution* (London 1978), p. 104.

14 Kate Millett, *Sexual Politics* (London 1977), p. 363.

15 Mary Daly, 'After the death of God the father', *Womanspirit Rising,* Christ and Plaskow op. cit., pp. 53-4.

16 ibid., pp. 54-5.

17 ibid., p. 54.

18 Mary Daly, 'The Qualitative Leap beyond Patriarchal Religion', *Quest* I (1974), p. 21.

19 In Christ and Plaskow, op. cit., p. 137.

20 Christ and Plaskow, op. cit., p. 147.

21 Susan Dowell and Linda Hurcombe, *Dispossessed Daughters of Eve* (London 1981), p. 113.

22 Sara Maitland, *A Map of the New Country* (London 1975), p. 109.

23 'Female Rites'; programme 1 of *Behind the Veil,* op. cit., LWT, 21 February 1982.

24 In Christ and Plaskow, op. cit., p. 147.

25 Rosemary Radford Ruether, *New Woman, New Earth* (New York 1975), p. 79.

26 Naomi Goldenberg, *Changing of the Gods* (Boston 1979), p. 4.

27 ibid., p. 5.

28 Catharina Halkes, 'The Themes of Protest in Feminist Theology against

God the Father', in J-B Metz and E. Schillebeeckx (eds.), 'God as Father' (*Concilium* 143, New York 1981), p. 105.

29 Christ and Plaskow, op. cit., p. 273.

30 ibid., p. 260.

31 Mary Daly, *Beyond God the Father: towards a philosophy of Women's Liberation* (Boston 1973), p. 96.

32 Susan Dowell, 'The Trinity is Two Men and a Question Mark', *Guardian*, 2 September 1982.

33 ibid.

34 Halkes, op. cit., p. 109.

35 Linda Clark, Marian Clark and Eleanor Walker, (eds.), *Image Breaking, Image Building* (New York 1981), pp. 47-8.

36 K. Marx, 'Contribution to the Critique of Hegel's Philosophy of Right', repr. *Marx and Engels on Religion*, Moscow 1957.

37 Christ and Plaskow, op. cit., p. 282. See also pp. 283ff.

38 Clark, Ronan and Walker, op. cit., p. 9.

39 ibid., p. 8.

40 Metz and Schillebeeckx, op. cit., p. vii.

41 ibid., pp. 103-9.

42 Rosemary Ruether, 'A Religion for Women: Sources and Strategies', *Christianity and Crisis* XXXIX, No. 19 (10 December 1979), pp. 307-11.

43 Metz and Schillebeeckx, op. cit., p. 108.

44 ibid., p. 64.

45 ibid., p. 66.

46 General Synod *Report of Proceedings* VI (1-2), 1975, pp. 572-3.

47 Paul Moore Jr., *Take a Bishop like Me* (New York 1979), p. 8.

48 ibid., p. 9.

49 ibid., p. 34.

50 ibid., p. 35.

51 ibid., p. 37.

52 Goldenberg, op. cit., pp. 8-9.

53 Lewis, op. cit., p. 91.

54 ibid., pp. 93-4.

PART TWO

Male and Female

Arriving alongside the emergency boat, someone spoke out of the darkness, and said, 'There are men in that boat.' I jumped in, and regret to say that there actually were. . . . They hopped out mighty quickly, and I encouraged them verbally, also by vigorously flourishing my revolver.   **Charles H. Lightoller**[1]

Senator Smith: From what you have said, you discriminated entirely in the interest of the passengers - first women and children - in filling these lifeboats?
Mr Lightoller: Yes, Sir.
Senator Smith: Why did you do that? Because of the captain's orders, or because of the rule of the sea?
Mr Lightoller: The rule of human nature.
                      U.S. Senate inquiry into the sinking of the *Titanic*[2]

It is a clear and consistent biblical assumption that men and women are not, in Bishop Michael Marshall's words, 'the same thing with different fittings';[3] that their biological differences correspond to clear differences of spiritual identity. All civilizations have believed this, or something like it. And in all societies, this perception of an essential spiritual, as well as merely biological, difference between the sexes has been reflected in a clear delineation of their social roles and in distinctive ways of behaving.

The way in which the sexes can be seen to differ is not, of course, always the same in different cultures, and from the fact that, for instance, in a small number of primitive societies some normal tendencies are claimed to have been reversed by cultural conditioning, feminists sometimes deduce that such differences are merely social constructs, artifically installed, which ought therefore to be eliminated. As we shall see, this is not the view of the anthropologists on whose work this argument tends most heavily to rely. At this stage, though, the most salient fact to register, simple but of overwhelming importance, is that however it may be observed, all known human societies without exception have assumed a clear distinction between 'masculine' and 'feminine' personality, behaviour and social roles.

5

The Feminist Challenge

It is the obsessive purpose of 'women's studies' and of feminist ideology to attempt to demonstrate that such distinctions have no necessary basis in human nature, and to establish a society in which they no longer exist. Thus, for Dr Una Kroll, 'the concepts of "feminine" and "masculine" (femininity/masculinity) [are] sexist in that they imprison human beings in sex-linked roles'. The only acceptable discrimination is the unavoidable biological difference: ' "female" and "male" take account of the proper distinction between free women and men'.[4] It is a familiar, even classic, expression of a fundamental feminist position. It is, perhaps, *the* fundamental feminist position even, paradoxically perhaps, for matriarchalist or 'pro-woman' feminism. It is the starting point: until this presupposition is accepted, the entire feminist enterprise has no point of intellectual departure.

And here, for feminists, is the great dilemma. Quite simply, the movement's basic assumption flies in the face of what has been, virtually without question until recent times, supposed by all human societies. Attempts, such as those made in the *kibbutzim* to eliminate 'imprisonment' in sex-linked roles, even when tenaciously pursued, have all broken down. The obvious and generally held conclusion, that it is in some way in the nature of human societies to differentiate between the sexes in a more than merely biological way, presents for modern feminism a vast theoretical problem, the solution to which has been pursued with single-minded passion. The problem is twofold in its scope. First and most fundamentally, how is the universality of this belief, if it is *not* essential to human nature, to be explained? The second question flows from the first, and is for obvious reasons even more urgent, particularly for those feminists who have not taken the final steps into female separatism, but are still involved in the struggle to convert potential allies within society in general and organizations like the Church in particular. The question is less one of basic theory than of apologetic necessity: how can a start be made to convince the liberal middle-class intellectuals (male and female) who are their natural constituency that this revolutionary challenge to hitherto universal beliefs does not do violence to simple common sense and observed reality? The question is less unsympathetically phrased than may appear. It is, after all, not dissimilar to the apologetic problem faced by religious people when they try to convince materialists that there is a reality beyond what can be seen and proved. But where the Church tries to convince the world that nearly all previous societies have been right, feminists argue that they have all, on a matter so close to the instinctual basis of the way in which human lives are actually lived, been quite wrong.

One solution to the problem is simply to claim for feminism what seems to be a version of what is already acceptable to most people, though semantically adjusted so that it can lead into more unequivocal feminist utterance; and to represent non-feminist opinion - if at all - by a crude, even silly, version of common belief. So, according to Kroll, 'there are no personality characteristics which are linked with a particular sex':[5] this, presumably, means that we cannot, for instance, say that only men are 'aggressive' and only women are 'tender' (this is, of course, undeniable); what we *can* say, Kroll continues, is that 'because they are "female" and "male", women and men use human characteristics in different ways': men and women are aggressive or tender in ways that are respectively male and female. It is strategically necessary at this point to avoid clarity: for of course, this is simply to say that males behave in a masculine way and females in a feminine way. Dr Kroll now goes on to complete the ploy with its optional second half, the misrepresentation of normal belief. 'I cannot imagine', she continues, 'that women and men correspond to the fantasy of being opposites of each other' (neither, of course can most non-feminists), 'instead I see them as complementary'. This she elaborates by suggesting, again unexceptionably, that 'women have a nurturing role and men a supportive one', and that 'neither quality is the exclusive property of one sex'.[6]

It is unclear how these views are consistent with a rejection of 'sex-linked roles', and certainly, at this point, Kroll would be decisively repudiated by many feminist writers, though not by all. Herbert Marcuse hoped that, through the women's liberation movement, qualities traditionally regarded as specifically feminine, like caring and gentleness, would be diffused through society, (though as a Marxist he supposed these feminine qualities to be socially determined).[7] Feminists, as Margaret Stacey and Marion Price comment in their survey *Women, Power and Politics* (1981), have frequently accepted some such paradoxical assumption, and a conference on 'Women and Elites', which took place at King's College, London, in 1980, was held on the hypothesis that, if women were integrated into the structures of power, 'if women joined the élites, the quality of those élites would change because of the specifically feminine contribution'.[8] Most radical feminists, however, have come to the view that, if women are to achieve real power, a more profound social and political revolution than any so far achieved must first take place: if sex-role differentiation is socially determined, then society itself must change radically before it can be eliminated. As Stacey and Price put it, if

> . . . 'feminine characteristics' are not biologically determined or universally present among womankind, they are closely associated with particular social roles that women have played. In order for the entry of women into the political arena to affect the way politics are played other changes are necessary: the nature of competitive society has also to change, relationships of domination and subordination in the factory and the workplace have to be removed, and men have to become involved in the nurturant roles . . .[9]

This elimination of sexually determined roles would take place as part of a wider revolution, which would involve changes in fundamental values leading in Kate Millet's words to 'a gathering impetus towards freedom from rank or pre-scriptive role, sexual or otherwise'.[10] The aim is nothing less than 'to transform personality', which, Millet goes on to say, 'cannot be done without freeing humanity from the tyranny of sexual social category and conformity to sexual stereotype - as well as abolishing racial caste and economic class.' Una Kroll, like most feminists, accepts this parallel with economic and racial oppression, and urges a transformation of the founda-tions of 'patriarchal' society; and she approvingly quotes Mary Daly's analysis, that 'women who are attempting to challenge the structures, values, and symbols of Christianity are at times not radical and daring enough, stopping at the goal of mere reforming within pre-established social structures . . .'[11]

Unlike Daly, however, Kroll (with her apparent - and somewhat puzzling - acceptance of a 'complementary' re-lationship between the sexes) does not perceive the logical end of the social revolution she urges. The 'self-transformation and spiritual rebirth' of the feminist brave new world, as Daly expresses it elsewhere,

> . . . involves the becoming of psychic unity, which means that one does not have to depend upon another for 'complementarity' but *can love independently* [my emphasis] . . . such independence means the becoming of psychologically androgynous human beings, since the basic crippling 'complementarity' has been the false masculine/feminine polarity. Androgynous integrity and transformation will require that women cease to play the role of 'complement' and struggle to stand alone as free human beings.[12]

This longing for solitary viability, for freedom from 'dependence', is one of the characteristic marks of the feminist consciousness, and several feminist writers (notably Mitchell[13] and Stacey and Price[14]) have suggested that its development among women was closely related to - indeed originated in - the growth of capitalism and bourgeois individualism. This is confusing, of a movement which derives much of its conceptual ballast from the Marxism of the New Left, and we can note in passing a source of one of the many theoretical incoherences in feminist thinking. Bourgeois individualism is, of course, to be swept away in the new order; the 'ego-centred way of the *individualist*' is to wither, and it will be replaced by 'the way of the androgyne'[15] (i.e. hermaphrodite). This will happen whether individuals want it or not. As June Singer puts it in her book *Androgyny* (1977), 'the evolutionary development of human consciousness will proceed onward, spurred by mutation, risk-taking and planning whether or not specific individuals are willing participants in it.'[16]

Despite the Orwellian overtones of such writing, it is important to note that 'androgyny', though indeed revolutionary in a historical perspective, represents nevertheless a less radical strain in feminist thinking (and one more easy to package for non-feminist opinion) than that which fosters women's consciousness as a distinctive and separate contribution to social revolution. 'Androgyny' provides the theoretical basis, indeed, for much of the social policy and legislation which apparently mildly reformist feminists have installed in countries like Britain and America. Thus, the British Equal Opportunities Commission concerns itself not only with such matters as equal pay for equal work, but with the control of children's literature and the suppression of patterns of education and play which could help in the development of traditionally 'masculine' and 'feminine' characteristics and behaviour.[17]

'Pro-woman' or 'exclusionist' feminism is more obviously radical and has correspondingly less chance of effecting changes in society, though it has provided during the seventies and early eighties a useful smoke-screen, under cover of which androgynist encroachments could be presented as comparatively moderate. Androgyny, however, tends to be regarded with scorn by those feminists who regard man as the oppressor, and have come to reject any collaboration with him. Thus, looking back on her career in feminist theology, the Mary Daly of *Gyn/Ecology* (1978) repudiates her earlier advocacy of androgyny as 'conveying something like John Travolta and Farrah Fawcett-Majors [cinema stars of the period] scotch-taped together'; and at the same time she expunges from her vocabulary the word 'God', replacing it with 'Goddess', and affirms a consciously chosen and ideologically motivated lesbianism.[18] The aim is no longer a collaboration with the male sex in order to achieve 'human liberation', but a deliberately embraced female exclusiveness, a 'self-discovery' to be achieved by excluding men and their preoccupations.

The appeal of androgyny is particularly, perhaps, to those feminists who have experienced the limitations of traditional 'equal rights' feminism and wish to go further, but dislike the idea of a sex war (conceived by analogy with the Marxist class war) which is so prominent in the writings of feminists like Daly and Millett:[19] an ideology which for a Betty Friedan 'makes a woman apologize for loving her husband. . . .' Friedan's aim is a 'two-sex movement for human liberation' achieved by the androgynist means of blurring the distinctiveness of the sexes, by an end to the 'obsolete sex-roles, the feminine and masculine mystiques, which torment us mutually'.[20]

Despite its dangers and incoherences, this way of thinking, in the short term at least, may well be increasing rather than diminishing in its influence within western society as a whole, and particularly in America. As Professor Olive Banks concludes in *Faces of Feminism* (1981):

> The androgynous approach is by no means without serious weaknesses at the theoretical level, and may represent no more than an attempt to avoid the revolutionary confrontation inevitable in both Marxist and radical feminism. At the same time, by accepting the need for quite large changes in male/female roles, it avoids some of the difficulties that have increasingly become apparent in equal rights feminism. For this reason, it is likely to continue to be an important element in feminism, particularly in the United States, where Marxist feminism has remained un-developed. Indeed it is possible . . . that social and economic changes, irrespective of feminist pressures, are already pointing towards a more androgynous society.[21]

There is certainly scope for some theologically oriented consideration of this last possibility, with all its implications for a period in the Church's history in which Christian leaders have so often shown themselves anxious to achieve relevance by speedily reflecting secular tendencies of this kind rather than bringing to bear on them a distinctively Christian critical scrutiny. It is clear, though, that social and economic change cannot be appealed to as an explanation of feminist success during the sixties and seventies in establishing, for many among the western liberal intelligentsia the plausibility of an assumption about the relationship between the sexes which would, it is necessary to insist, have seemed grotesque to any previous age, and still seems so to most of the human race.

The theory, let us recall, is that there is no essential difference, apart from biology, between the sexes; that there is no basis apart from social conditioning for sexually differ-entiated roles within society; and that such differentiation ought *therefore* to be eliminated. How has the intellectual foundation of this hypothesis been constructed? One successful method has been by surveying the literature in a variety of fields, notably in sociology, psychology and anthropology, and using evidence thus garnered selectively though often per-suasively to arrive at the looked-for conclusion. This is one of the principal functions of 'women's studies', which tend on the whole not to present evidence incoherent with the feminist analysis, unless necessary for polemical ends. Their purpose is to present the feminist case: as Rosemary Ruether puts it, 'women's studies do not pretend to an ethical neutrality. This stance is actually a ruling class ideology. Neutrality hides a commitment to the status quo. All liberation scholarship is advocacy scholarship'.[22] If one field of study seems for the moment unsympathetic to feminist conclusions, it may simply be sidestepped by an appeal elsewhere: if, for instance, the conclusions of psychology will not serve, anthropology may come to the rescue. Thus Eva Figes, in *Patriarchal Attitudes* (1978): 'Everyone has to work their way through the Oedipal situation, declares Freud. Pardon me, answers Malinowski, but in the place where I work families do not recognize the father figure, so the situation simply never arises in the first place. Exit Freud'.[23]

This is, however, a perilous procedure: the Malinowski of *Sex and Repression in Savage Society* (1927), used as a stick to beat Freud, may be directly contradicted by a later Malinowski, used by another feminist writer as an authority on the universally patriarchal character of all societies. Here is Kate Millett quoting from *Sex, Culture and Myth* (1962) (to illustrate 'how basic a form patriarchy is within all societies') Malinowski's 'principle of legitimacy': that 'no child should be brought into the world without a man - and one man at that - assuming the role of sociological father'. This principle, concludes Millett, is 'consistent and universal'.[24]

This kind of juggling with snippets of scholarly lore by no means represents the final solution of the problem of recalcitrant academic opinion. Any field of study which seems to provide conclusions consistently unsympathetic to the feminist analysis can always be written off as male dominated: thus psychology can become simply '*male* psychology', and any conclusions drawn by male psychologists about differences between the sexes simply discounted: only study of women by women, and in a feminist context, can be accepted as unbiased. Thus, for Joanna Bunker Rohrbaugh:

the view of women has been so distorted in traditional *male psychology* that it bears only a slight resemblance to real life. Only when women have been studied separately, and have begun to define themselves apart from men, can we come to any realistic understanding of how and why the two sexes really differ.[25]

This in itself is, of course, a highly artificial and value-laden suggestion, since the view under attack is precisely that neither sex *can* be studied apart from the other.

Such considerations, however, are of little moment: knowledge, for feminist writers, is there principally to be *used*. Such information as seems valuable may be removed from its general context in its field and deployed, without reference either to views which may cast doubt on it, or even, as we have seen, to the general conclusions of the scholar whose work is being used in this way. Perhaps the most vivid example of this kind of abuse can be observed in the conclusions drawn from, and the weight attached to, the findings of the anthropologist Margaret Mead among three neighbouring tribes, published in *Sex and Temperament in Three Primitive Societies* (1935). In one tribe, Mead found both sexes passive, co-operative and non-aggressive. In another, river dwellers, both men and women appeared ruthless and lacking in tenderness. In a third, lake dwellers, Mead observed the women as dominant and the men as economically and sexually dependent. Her conclusion from this early fieldwork (quoted as authoritative by Figes)[26] was that 'the evidence is overwhelmingly in favour of strength of social conditioning' as the principal source of sex-role differentiation. Rohrbaugh admits that 'of course, the evidence from these small tribes cannot be interpreted as showing that a broad pattern of sex difference in personality and social roles does not exist across cultures.' The point at issue, says Rohrbaugh, is raised by the evidence that normal patterns can be reversed: this shows that they 'cannot be based purely or even primarily on intrinsic or biological sex differences.'[27] From this point, the way is open for the desired conclusion. If there is *some* evidence that there exist *some* cultures in which normal patterns have been reversed, and that normal patterns are themselves established in Malinowski's words as part of a 'building up of complex and artificial habit responses,'[28] it follows from this (so goes the androgynist line) that these patterns are open to being reorganized in any way a given society decides, and that sex differences should *therefore* be programmed out of all human societies as soon as this can be arranged. This will, of course, take time and will encounter sexist obstruction. But the goal has been defined and is now arguably attainable.

Three observations may be made on this argument, and on the way in which it deploys specific evidence. First, no attempt is made here, or in other feminist writings where this particular work of Mead's is cited, to confirm, or establish the status of, Mead's findings. And yet, *Sex and Temperament in Three Primitive Societies* is, for Rohrbaugh, 'the classic evidence,'[29] and is cited by Figes as one of three works 'particularly valuable for us'.[30] In fact, though recent work has questioned the accuracy of Mead's early observations among primitive peoples particularly severely, it is also true that, as one anthropologist puts it, Margaret Mead 'does not and never has exemplified for anthropologists the highest standards of ethnographic field research'.[31]

Secondly, even if it could be accepted that the findings are solid, and that Rohrbaugh and others soundly draw from them conclusions as to the *possibility* of broad and transcultural patterns of sex differentiation being eliminated, this cannot establish that it would be *desirable* to do so. Whatever the truth of Mead's observations about these primitive peoples, it is significant that such 'reversals' have not been characteristic of any advanced civilisation.

Thirdly, the conclusions of Mead herself,[32] particularly in her mature later work, run directly counter to those drawn by Rohrbaugh and others, who carefully ignore the general context of the development of Mead's work on sex differentiation. Though *Male and Female* (1947) is sometimes quoted to show (undeniable) variations between cultures, its conclusion that sex-role differentiation has biological as well as sociological origins is, with one very notable exception (that of Betty Friedan), usually ignored.[33] Since it is impossible to imagine a modern feminist who has not read Friedan, it must be assumed that this silence is deliberate.

The final relevance of questions of whether the distinct social roles played in all societies by men and women reflect innate differences, of the part played in the formation of these roles by society itself, and of whether human societies could actually function without them, is probably, indeed, best summed up by Mead herself, in a passage quoted by Friedan to demonstrate her apostasy, a passage in which Mead goes on to open up a further question particularly suggestive for theological reflection. 'We are dealing here', she says,

> . . . with two individual questions: are we dealing not with a *must* that we dare not flout because it is rooted so deep in our biological mammalian nature that to flout it means individual and social disease? or with a *must* that, although not so deeply rooted, still is so very socially convenient and so well tried that it would be uneconomical to flout it . . . But there is still the third possibility. Are not sex differences exceedingly valuable, one of the resources of our human nature that every society has used but no society has as yet begun to use to the full?[34]

6
'Misogyny' and the Jewish Inheritance

It is particularly useful to begin from this general perspective, one concerned with observations carried out in a wide variety of cultural environments, since much attention has been devoted to pointing out that biblical teaching on the relations between the sexes is deeply rooted in one particular 'patriarchal' culture, that of the Jews up to and including St Paul. In general, this is held by feminist writers to disqualify it from serious consideration except for polemical purposes. The perception, not only that there are many ways in which women were and are especially valued in the Hebrew tradition, but also that much of the biblical understanding of sex differentiation is, in its broad lines, common to many cultures, and in some important respects to all, helps us to perceive that the ancient Hebrews are not thus easily to be shuffled off with all their cultural baggage as too barbarous and remote for their beliefs to be relevant to the concerns of men and women today.

It seems to be essential, however, to the Christian feminist case (is, at least, a normal part of it) to attempt to establish that Jewish society over the relevant period was based not simply on male authority (this is, of course clear enough, and is equally true of nearly all other known cultures) but on a systematic installation of female inferiority, even degradation, characteristic of this and other 'patriarchal' cultures (but not, in some versions, of the 'matriarchal' cultures they are held to have supplanted).[35] The Jewish tradition is innately misogynist (so runs this argument); this misogyny was inherited by Christianity from its Jewish origins - particularly through St Paul - and confirmed by Hellenistic influences as the Christian movement spread through the ancient world.

We shall not consider in any detail the incorrect assumptions that 'matriarchal' religions involved a higher status for women in society, and that at some stage matriarchal political structures actually existed and were displaced by patriarchy,[36] though we shall pay some attention to feminist methods of biblical exegesis at a later stage. First, however, it is necessary to touch on one key area for feminist deployment of biblical and anthropological material: the position of women in the cultic life of Israel, and the cultic regulations surrounding female sexuality. Particularly, we need to consider the 'exclusion' of women from the conduct of public worship and the regulations concerning ritual 'uncleanness' involved in menstruation and childbirth; these regulations, in particular, provide an often cited body of 'evidence' for the disgust and fear allegedly aroused in men by female sexuality (sometimes referred to as 'body hatred', or even 'cunt hatred'):[37] for Dowell and Hurcombe, 'the hallmark of male supremacist society to this day.[38] And since these cultic regulations are still observed by orthodox Jewish women, it will be interesting to elicit whether later Rabbinic exegesis, and contemporary understanding, demonstrate a consistent basis of 'misogyny' or not.

The Hebrew 'taboo' against menstrual fluid (like other such 'primitive taboos') ascribed, according to Rosemary Ruether, a demonic character to sexual fluids, primarily female. This concept of uncleanness is used to segregate adult women for most of their lives, and forbid them access to male precincts of sacerdotal, political, and educational power.[39]

And the ritual uncleanness of menstruant women in Hebrew religion developed, according to Ruether, 'as maternal power was denigrated and suppressed culturally'.[40] This 'primitive taboo' remains, even in modern industrial society, a means of suppressing women: 'feminists and non-feminists alike', claim Dowell and Hurcombe, 'recognize the extent to which the ritual uncleanness of menstruation still subconsciously applies to women in our own culture.'[41]

How much the idea of the disgust and fear allegedly aroused among male 'supremacists' by female biology, rather than deriving from the supposedly dark and perverse nature of a remote and ancient people is actually a projection from our own sanitized and deodorized culture, transmitted by the modern feminist psyche, with its often aggressive concern to conquer and contain female biology in the quest for liberation, may well be a question worth asking. What we need to explain, more urgently than ancient Hebrew religion, is how a writer like Rosemary Ruether can with impunity present such a parody of the facts, and why she feels the need to do so. There is, in fact, no question of the ancient Hebrews ascribing 'a demonic character to sexual fluids', male or female. The purification rites prescribed after menstruation (like those after childbirth, and indeed all Hebrew cleansing rituals) were quite unlike pagan lustrations which, says Yehezkel Kaufmann, were 'designed to protect men and gods from the demonic or magical action of impurity'. But: 'the Bible preserves *no trace* of this idea'. On the contrary:

> In spite of its belief in the substantiality of impurity, the Bible does not accord to it the status of a primary, demonic force. There is no tension of powers between the holy and the impure. Impurity is no more than a condition - one might almost say a religious aesthetic state. . . . In contrast to the pagan conception impurity is in itself not a source of danger; its divine-demonic roots have been totally destroyed.[42]

Nor does the inhibition against sexual activity during menstruation because of the woman's ritual impurity in any way imply male repugnance or contempt, and there is a convenient way of verifying this. Whatever the meaning of Dowell and Hurcombe's dark insinuations that 'the ritual uncleanness of menstruation still subconsciously applies to women in our own culture', there are of course still some women in our own culture to whom it applies not only subconsciously but in actual practice as well. Is it, for *them*, a source of humiliation and exclusion? Apparently not: as one Orthodox rabbi's wife explained in the *Behind the veil* television series, the days of abstention

> . . . raise the status of the woman in marriage, because sex is no longer dependent on one partner's whim all the time, and there's a feeling that God's there as well; and a lot of the abuses that one gets the feeling can exist in a marriage really can be moved out . . . also it means a relationship has to be real, because the relationship has to be worked out at a proper level.[43]

Certainly, if we seek for an authentic modern understanding of this ancient practice we will probably be wiser to do so from the context of the Jewish religion itself, than from the perspective of a Christian feminist polemic whose principal purpose is to diagnose 'misogyny' wherever it can within the Judaeo-Christian tradition. The preservation of the Jewish menstrual laws, with all their restrictions, after the disappearance of the sacrificial system with which they had been associated, was undoubtedly not due to their ever having been useful for the 'suppression' of women, nor even because they had become inseparably associated with sexual habit or for any supposed 'hygienic' reason. Their persistence has a more positive basis, as Professor Raphael Loewe explains:

> It is rather a conscious emphasis on, and an attempt at the inculcation in a particularly significant area of human interest, of that self-discipline which must be - in all aspects of life - an integral element in the Jewish ideal of cultivating 'holiness' (*qedushah*).[44]

The laws of ritual purity now apply mainly to women, through menstruation (as we have seen) and also in connection with childbirth: here, too, it is necessary to stress that there is no question of purification involving any neutralizing of danger or evil. It is rather a question of bringing that which has had contact with the *holy* back into the ambit of everyday life, in the same sense that contact with the scrolls of the Torah was held in ancient tradition to 'soil the hands', or in the Christian liturgy, as the priest speaks of 'purifying' the chalice and ciborium which have contained the sacred elements.[45] The almost exclusive modern application of the ritual purity laws to women is thus seen as the opposite of a discrimination *against* them; on the contrary, as Dr Jonathan Webber puts it, they 'are thus given the main opportunity (or the honour) of preserving this element or idiom of religious holiness'.[46]

And here, perhaps, is a vital clue. Where some modern western Christians tend to see such laws as negative in their effect on women, the Orthodox Jewish tradition genuinely tends to see them as positive. Where such Christians see 'restrictions' and 'exclusions', the Jew genuinely sees 'opportunities', and 'exemptions', even 'privileges'.[47] The same is true of Jewish spirituality: thus, the prayer of the Jewish male (much quoted by feminists) in which he blesses God for not being a heathen, a slave, or a woman, is *not* seen as an occasion on which he can stand daily before God to celebrate his superiority over the female sex, and it must be said that this feminist interpretation (surely hardly believable even without a knowledge of the facts) assumes a curious, even grotesque view of the purpose of prayer for the devout Jew. The three classes of person mentioned were all, of course, exempt from the obligation of the time-bound spiritual disciplines incumbent on the Jewish male, and the purpose of this particular set of blessings (part of a long series) is to thank God for having made him a being thus constrained, 'for having been vouchsafed the opportunity', as Loewe puts it, 'for a more active and intense (though not necessarily in each case "higher") spiritual activity than would have been the case had the accident of birth been otherwise.'[48] Women are, of course, taught to bless God for having made *them* as *they* are: 'Blessed art thou, O Lord our God, King of the Universe, who hast made me according to thy will.'[49] And that this female nature is *not* seen in the Jewish tradition as one of invincible inferiority to that of the male is hardly difficult to show. As the Talmud asserts, their exemption from the time-bound obligations, incumbent on the males, for the conduct of the synagogue liturgy and the observance of other disciplines, implies, in Moshe Meiselmann's words, 'nothing as to the relative worth of male and female - both are equally sacred'.[50] Some later authorities, indeed, have seen these exemptions as evidence of the greater ease with which women achieve spiritual goals. The Maharal of Prague explains that man's aggressiveness deflects him from his spiritual objectives, and that he must therefore be given extra religious obligations. Woman's nature is instrinsically closer to the serenity required for spiritual growth, and it is even assumed that they will generally attain a higher spirituality.[51] Rabbi Samson Raphael Hirsch insists that the Torah did not impose the time-bound disciplines on women, 'because it did not consider them necessary to be demanded from women':

> God's Torah takes it for granted that our women have greater fervour and more faithful enthusiasm for their God-serving calling and that their calling runs less danger in their case than in that of men . . . Accordingly, it does not find it necessary to give women those repeated spurring reminders to remain true to their calling . . .[52]

Are we then, to see the Jewish tradition as being one consistently *favourable* to women? The question, thus posed in uncompromisingly modern 'egalitarian' terms, is probably as meaningless as its converse. Examination, for instance, of the legal and institutional position (which derives from Pentateuchal law) provides no clear answer either way. Webber, confirming Loewe, discerns four different kinds of material in the Jewish legal code, in which women are (a) not significantly differentiated, (b) seem to be granted privileges, (c) seem to be discriminated against, (d) have specifically female-oriented rituals provided.[53]

The Old Testament as a whole presents the same lack of clear definition on this matter as the Torah. As we have seen, the exemption of women from the conduct of public worship is not seen as deriving from any spiritual inferiority; this is coherent with the fact that the transformation of the great prophetesses by the Spirit is perceived by the community, and their prophecy recognized as such, without any discernible sense of 'culture-shock'. Women play important roles in the history of the covenant, demonstrating - whether for good or ill in any particular case - their influence over the moral and religious life of their husbands. Certainly, the examples of Jezebel and the foreign women who turn the heart of Solomon toward their gods (1 Kings 11. 1-8) show the female sex in a bad light; but they also provide an insight into women's spiritual authority within the family.

And it is here that the most vivid picture emerges: the relationship of husband and wife is seen as one in which the husband is as emotionally dependent as the wife. A wife is a source of blessing and a sign of God's favour (Prov. 18.22); she is no mere chattel (as feminists consistently claim of the lot of the wife in the Old Testament) but a person with whom, in a properly functioning marriage, there will be a relationship of mutual love and esteem. Let your wife, advises the author of *Proverbs*,

> . . . your fountain be blessed, rejoice in the wife of your youth . . .
> Let her affection fill you at all times with delight . . . (Prov. 5.18-19)

'I am my beloved's and my beloved is mine' (Song of Sol. 2.16): this is not the relationship of owner and chattel. Nor, even, is the good wife like a kind of geisha, there for the husband's pleasure: 'If a man is newly married', prescribes Deuteronomy (24.5), 'he shall not join the army nor is he to be pestered at home; he shall be left at home free of all obligations for one year to bring joy to the wife that is taken.'

The ideal of the good wife in Hebrew and Jewish tradition is clear enough, and it is one by no means either falsely romanticized or otherwise demeaning to women: it is both tender and realistic. And it is worth pointing out that many of the sporadic outbursts of apparent misogyny in the Bible have to do with the man's dependence on woman for his happiness, and his vulnerability if the woman proves false (e.g. Delilah, Judg. 14.15ff) or foolish (Prov. 9.13-18) or quarrelsome:

A foolish son is ruin to his father, and a wife's quarrelling is a
   continual dripping of rain.
House and wealth are inherited from fathers; but a prudent wife is
   from the Lord.   (Prov. 19.13-14)

7
Culture and Belief

The simple fact that in the Jewish tradition men and women are
seen to have distinct roles in society and the family, quite as
much as that tradition's alleged degradation of women, is
enough to account for feminist distaste; and we can accept
without reluctance that this tradition undoubtedly - as
Christian feminists insistently point out - provides the soil
which nurtures Paul's own understanding of the relationship
between the sexes, even though at some points he clearly
redefines it. But before we approach the Pauline teaching we
need to think, with more clarity than is sometimes shown,
about the nature of the connection between culture and belief,
and particularly as this affects the relationship of men and
women. It is, of course, impossible to speak concretely of the
way in which the sexes relate to each other without referring to
particular cultures in which their relationship is rooted. And it
is undoubtedly true that the various strands of biblical teaching
on the relationship between the sexes are woven into the
developing social as well as religious understanding of the
Hebrew people. But this perception can lead to a number of
misapprehensions particularly damaging to clear thinking on
this issue, if we deduce simply that all such matters are
therefore 'relative' and that it is only the 'realities' of our
own society which carry weight as a serious factor in any discussion.

   First, it needs to be said that it is as much part of
fundamental Christian teaching as of Jewish teaching to see the
Jews as specially singled out by God for his purposes, and to
decribe them as 'the chosen people'. Their culture, therefore, is

in a real way the *chosen* culture, and its norms may consequently be in some vital aspects nearer reality than those of our own denatured and despiritualized civilization. Secondly, an understanding of what is characteristically 'of an age' may lead to an understanding of what is universal within its cultural expression. A close attention to the Elizabethan background of Shakespeare's plays, for instance, does not convince us of how ephemeral and culture-bound his perceptions are; on the contrary, it leads us further into the universality and massiveness of scale of his particular understanding of the human condition. So, too, with the great religious teachers, *including St Paul*; of whose writings it seems to be particularly necessary to insist that it is often the case that within culturally determined and contingent teachings there may lie eternal principles, of which we lose sight by locating textual meaning too precisely within its transient elements (adding as we do so that the transient elements are not necessarily those which are incongruous with the assumptions of our own culture). Paul's teachings, for instance, on the need for a woman's head to be covered in church (1 Cor. 11.5ff) and enjoining women's silence in the assembly (1 Cor.14.33ff) seem to be addressed to particular and ephemeral pastoral situations, and their authority *as practical advice* has as clearly now lapsed. But the principles with which Paul is truly concerned here, within the context of re-establishing right order within an actual congregation, are more important. As Karl Barth puts it, commenting on these two passages,

> The essential point is that woman must always and in all circumstances be woman; that she must feel and conduct herself as such and not as a man; that the command of the Lord, which is for all eternity, directs both man and woman to their own proper sacred place and forbids all attempts to violate this order. The command may be given a different interpretation from that of Paul, for it is the living command of the living Lord. Yet if it is to be respected at all it cannot even for a moment or in any conceivable sense be disregarded in this its decisive expression and requirement.[54]

And in directing the sexes to 'their proper sacred place', Barth says of 1 Cor. 14.33ff, 'appearances must be very deceptive . . . if he was really relegating them to an inferior position . . . the command of the Lord does not put anyone, man or woman, in a humiliating, dishonourable or unworthy position. It puts both man and woman in their proper place.'

8
Hierarchy and Equality

And here we are beginning to approach the peculiar difficulties, for the twentieth-century mind, in trying to identify what *is* the proper place of men and women within an authentically Christian order. For if it is undeniable that Paul's teachings are in some sense culturally contingent in their expression, mediated by a first-century mind attempting to make concrete a timeless gospel within actual first-century communities, it is equally true that we ourselves are even more constrained by the more assertive and more mechanistic ethos of our own century: it is necessary to insist that in some real respects Paul's horizons were less spiritually constricted than our own. At the very least we are entitled to say, in the words of Dr Graham Leonard that 'the exercise of a critical Christian judgement compels us to ask how far in our understanding of the New Testament documents we are conditioned by the culture and society of our time', and with him to add that 'there is no intrinsic reason why it should be given an authority which is denied to that of any one age.'[55]

We need, then, to be very careful when we dismiss teachings which may seem to be irrelevant and culturally limited or even unjust, but which may be so only to minds confined within a civilization like our own, in which human beings appear to themselves enlightened and increasingly free, but in which they are in fact in so many ways enthralled in a profound ignorance about the very basis of human dignity and freedom; an ignorance all the darker for seeming to be knowledge. One obvious example of the singularity of our society can be seen in the idea, entertained by many within it, that freedom, or 'liberation', is to be attained by (among other specifics) the abolition of social and political structures in which the exercise of *authority* is a necessary part. This can be seen vividly reflected within the Church in a hostility (endemic in Christian feminism and in the Christian new left generally) towards its 'hierarchical' structures. It needs to be said clearly that - whatever may be said about injustice and oppression - the quest for freedom from patterns of authority which involve the subordination of some human beings to others, whether within the Church itself, within the family, or within society at large, cannot be seen to be any significant part of the Christian tradition or of biblical teaching. The reverse is in fact the case, and this is true of the Christian movement from its earliest days. The 'elders' of the early Church can be seen as the equivalents of the powerful Jewish elders of the first century; in the Church the elders were described also as bishops, and performed the same functions of ruling, judging, and teaching.[56] The bishop was a pastor, and his authority was not to be used oppressively (1 Pet. 5.1-3); relationships of authority and subordination were, nevertheless, clearly seen as a necessary part of a properly functioning Christian community from the very beginning (1 Tim. 5.17; 1 Thess. 5.12; Heb. 13.17, 24).[57]

The same is true of Christian teaching on the secular political order. Earthly structures of authority are to be not abolished but redeemed, their meaning transmuted in the perspective of God's own authority, and by the incorporation of individuals subject to them into Christ. This does not rule out the possibility of a secular order so demonic that a Christian should disobey it: but the assumption is that in normal circumstances the Christian redefinition of social relationships will operate at a different level. Even the extreme case of the institution of slavery itself (the structural abolition of which has not, historically, always led to the abolition of its spirit) can, in its concrete expression, actually cease to be demonic if master and slave now see their relationship in the light of Christ: the actual granting of a freedom operating on the socio-political plane may then become almost irrelevant. St Paul, in sending back to his master Philemon the runaway slave Onesimus, now a

Christian, sends him back 'for good, no longer as a slave, but as more than a slave - as a dear brother, very dear indeed to me and how much more to you, both as a man and as a Christian' (Phil. 15-16). But their earthly relationship of master and slave (surprisingly for our modern expectations) is, so far as we can see, to remain, not abolished but in a vital way made part of the divine order: slaves, says Paul elsewhere, should be obedient to their masters, 'rendering service with a good will as to the Lord and not to men' (Eph. 6.7; see also 1 Cor. 7.20-23; Col. 3.22-5; 1 Tim. 6.1-2; Titus 2.9; 1 Pet. 2.18-25). It is a revolutionary redefinition, infinitely more radical than any mere political readjustment could ever be. This does *not* of course mean that the abolition of slavery becomes an irrelevant political question. But it does mean that the truly radical change must be one in the hearts of men, otherwise structural and political change is profitless. More importantly for our inquiry, it shows us how, within the community of the redeemed, a radical equality can coexist with a subordinate relationship.

It is in some such way that we must preface any inquiry as to how, in the late twentieth century, and in all likelihood setting out from the preconceptions of the western bourgeois intelligentsia, we are to understand the Pauline texts which touch on the relationship between the sexes, above all if we are to perceive their entire internal consistency. To understand how equality can be consistent with subordination on the one hand, and the exercise of authority on the other, demands a radical distancing of our normal secular expectations, and an openness to the way in which all our relationships are transformed inside the fifth dimension of life within the resurrection community. This is, emphatically, *not* to 'spiritualize' Paul's message in some unacceptable gnostic sense, in which the world is simply written off as unredeemable: but it *is* to assert that all our relationships are now to be seen *sub specie aeternitatis*, that we are beings, in Jesus' words, 'not of the world' (John 17.16), for whom all existing human expectations now assume a new significance. We are in the world, with all the responsibilities and tensions that entails; but we are, nevertheless, in an essential way, not *of* it. To be a Christian is to live with paradox; to be seen 'as unknown, and yet well-known; as dying, and behold we live . . . as having nothing, and yet possessing everything' (2 Cor. 9-10).

Within such a dispensation, the authority normally exercised by men in society and within the family is transformed from the crude, coercive domination it can be in a fallen and disordered world, into an entirely new principle of human relationship: the authority of the crucified Christ, now mediated by his Church, and within the Christian family particularly by the father. But no one is exempt from Christ's own subjection; we are to accept a kind of mutual subordination. The wife is subject to the husband; and the husband, if necessary, is to die for the wife. Ephesians 5.21ff, a key Pauline passage here, should be quoted at some length:

> Be subject to one another out of reverence for Christ. Wives, be subject to your husbands, as to the Lord. For the husband is the head of the wife as Christ is the head of the church, his body, and is himself its Saviour. As the church is subject to Christ, so let wives also be subject in everything to their husbands. Husbands, love your wives, as Christ loved the church, and gave himself up for her . . . Even so husbands should love their wives as their own bodies. He who loves his wife loves himself. For no man ever hates his own flesh, but nourishes and cherishes it, as Christ does the church, because we are members of his body. 'For this reason a man shall leave his father and mother and be joined to his wife, and the two shall become one flesh.' This is a great mystery, and I take it to mean Christ and the church; however, let each one of you love his wife as himself, and let the wife see that she respects her husband.

Undoubtedly, this balance of love, obedience, obligation and sacrifice has not, within Christian civilization, always been observed. What is perhaps more striking, however, is how unquestioned in practice its acceptance has often been. The sinking of the *Titanic* remains as a kind of modern icon of the assertion of sacrificial and Christ-like male authority over the female within the Christian dispensation: perhaps some of the successful and powerful male 'supremacists', who died so that their wives and daughters might live, remembered as they calmly awaited death, the prayer (based on Ephesians 5) which the parson had read at the marriage ceremonies of many of them: 'Look mercifully upon these thy servants, that both this man may love his wife, according to thy word (as Christ did love his spouse the Church, who gave himself for it . . .) and also that this woman may be loving and amiable, faithful and obedient to her husband . . .'[58] To Charles H. Lightoller, one of the sailors put in charge of the lifeboats full of women and children, their priority over the men in such a situation seemed, quite simply, 'the law of human nature.'[59] Whether, in the context of some other traditions, it would have seemed so may be open to question. Even more, we may ask whether, some seventy years later, such distinctions of sex would still be asserted: and if they would not, whether such a development towards an androgynous society genuinely represents an advance for human civilization, or a regression into barbarism.

Within the context of Ephesians 5.21ff, thus understood, the apparent dissonance between Paul's repeated insistence on the headship of the man over the woman, in the family and in the community, and his no less clear assertion of their equality within the Christian dispensation, begins to resolve itself:

> . . . in Christ Jesus you are all sons of God, through faith. For as many of you as were baptized into Christ have put on Christ. There is neither Jew nor Greek, there is neither slave nor free, there is neither male nor female; for you are all one in Christ Jesus. (Gal. 3.26-8)

Such a resolution, however, is not helpful to the feminist cause, and the 'inconsistency' of Paul's teaching is asserted and explained in various ways. Passages in feminist terms 'favourable' to women are to be preserved; and various ways of detaching them from Paul's other teachings on the relationship between the sexes are offered. According to Fiorenza,[60] for instance, the central Galatians passage just quoted is actually a pre-Pauline baptismal confession, which Paul employs to promote his view that Jews and Gentiles are to be accepted on equal terms. The reference to male and female thus insinuates itself, undigested, into the Pauline teaching, which it may now be used to refute. Isolating Galatians 3.26ff does not deal with the problem, of course, since this is hardly the only 'pro-woman' passage in Paul. 1 Cor. 11.11-12, for instance, asserts that 'in the Lord woman is not independent of man nor man of woman; for as woman was made from man, so man is now born of woman. And all things are from God.' But this comes after one of the best-known assertions (in 1 Cor. 11.3ff) of man's headship, and is clearly meant to be part of the same argument. How are these teachings to be detached from one another? Robert Hamerton-Kelly's solution is to suggest a view of a Paul torn between opposing views. 'It is as though', he writes, 'having set out on an impossible mission - to justify the "sign of authority" on women - he wishes the whole argument would self-destruct'. And so, 'his good sense and Christian conscience reassert themselves and Paul throws up his hands . . .'[61]

The key to perceiving the consistency of Paul's teaching seems to be that we must always try to understand him theologically. It is noticeable that the feminist exegesis which attenuates Paul normally does so by imposing modern secular expectations on to the text, thus representing Paul's writings (where they are inconvenient to the feminist view) as 'culturally contingent' but, where they seem useful, as deriving also from his revolutionary inspiration, from a message of which - culture-bound as he was - he could not absorb the largely cultural implications. As Constance Parvey puts the argument, 'though a gifted visionary, theologian, teacher and organizer, he was not a social reformer in the modern sense. Like other men of genius, he found it difficult to adapt his social thought to conform with his radically new theology.'[62] In other words, Paul *ought* to have been a social reformer, because his 'radically new theology' (so it seems to be implied) is significant chiefly as an instrument of social change.[63] To assert against this a more theological understanding is not to 'spiritualize' the argument: it is to say that Paul's principal concern is with the achievement of a right relationship, within an authentically ordered Christian community, of men and women with God; and that it is only within this God-centred priority that his writings on community in its concrete manifestations can be approached. This seems an obvious enough perception, in all conscience. It needs to be registered, nevertheless, if we are to cope adequately with such texts as 1 Cor. 11.3: '. . . what I want you to understand is that Christ is the head of every man, man is the head of woman, and God is the head of Christ.' We have seen in Ephesians 5.21ff, Paul's teaching on the sacrificial authority of the husband within marriage and on the mutual love and dependence of husband and wife; here Paul explains the relationship of man and woman within the Christian community at large. As in the family, man is the head of woman, and woman is not therefore to usurp his function within this order. But this does *not* imply a relationship between them which is degrading to the woman (and to say this is not to deny that there have been those who have misinterpreted Paul, with baneful consequences). As Roger Beckwith puts it:

> If the woman is subordinate to the man, the man is subordinate to Christ, which is no degrading relationship; moreover Christ is subordinate to God (the Father), and there is nothing degrading in the internal relationships of the Holy Trinity. This teaching about the subordination of the Son to the Father is one to which Paul returns later in the epistle (1 Cor. 15.27ff); it is a subordination wholly consistent with the unity and equality of nature between the Father and the Son; and it provides the highest possible model for the relationship between the sexes.

But to understand equality in *this* way, it is necessary entirely to distance ourselves from any merely human or ephemerally political understanding of the word. Our relationships are 'in Christ'; and to *prefer*, or give priority to, any non-theological understanding, rooted in twentieth-century western culture, is not to be *more* radical, but to be infinitely *less* so. This, with a vengeance, is to enclose the Christian message within cultural horizons of man's own making; a procedure whose dangers we do not need to look far into history to perceive. As Karl Barth wrote to Henrietta Visser 't Hooft in 1934, '. . . a great many Christians in Germany today object to the fact that Christ was a Jew. Time will show whether their objections are salutary. And women can object to the fact that the Bible says that "man is the woman's head". Time will show whether it is good to reverse this disposition or (as you would like to do) to neutralize it.' And Barth continues: '. . . there is another possibility: not to oppose God's dispositions but to accept them without argument because they *are*, and then perhaps with time to realize that they are *good*.'[65]

9

The Teaching of Christ

Barth's position here is, of course, based on the assumption of the Christian Church through the ages that Paul's teaching and practice is not merely *congruous* with that of Jesus himself, but that he in a unique way speaks with Christ's own commission. When Paul speaks, it is Jesus who speaks through him; and it is significantly in the context of the crucial teaching on the relationship between the sexes in 1 Corinthians 14 that he makes one of his great claims to this authority (v. 37). It is this claim above all that Christian feminist exegesis is concerned to deny. Paul may indeed (almost despite himself) convey authentic dominical teaching on a number of occasions, and these may be freely cited. But - so runs the argument - the weight of his misogynist Jewish background and temperament tends effectively to neutralize the revolutionary teaching and practice of Jesus himself. And so, almost uniquely in a reactionary Judaeo-Christian tradition, Jesus the feminist shines as a lonely beacon across the centuries, to inspire and illuminate the aspirations of modern Christian feminism.

Not only feminist writers, of course, have stressed the radical character of Jesus' understanding of the role of women, and the ways in which he diverges from orthodox contemporary Jewish practice. The question to be answered is *how* this redefinition can be seen to operate, and how precisely it differs from that of the early Church, particularly as we see it reflected in Paul's writings. Certainly, whatever Jesus may be argued to imply (or to deny) about the *distinctiveness* of the sexes, he does not accept the then current rabbinic teaching about their *separation* (a separation which had not existed in earlier Hebrew tradition).[66] Women are constantly in his company, on one occasion even privately - to the surprise of his returning disciples (John 4.27). He heals them, ignoring if necessary the ritual purity laws (Mark 5.25-34), and the inhibition against touching women (Matt. 8.14-15). The story of Martha and Mary shows that the gospel is for women too, and that there is no separate or distinct teaching for them. When he teaches, his parables contain examples from women's lives. They are 'daughters of Abraham' (Luke 13.6): and in the end, at the great climax of the Christian story, as the male authors of John (20.11-19) and Matthew (28.9-10) record, it is to women that Jesus first appears after his resurrection: they are the first witnesses (a role given them by Jesus, which they would have been denied in a Jewish court).

Much of this, without any doubt, represents a clear divergence from the belief and practice of those who strictly observed the teachings of the scribe-rabbis of first-century Judaism (a tradition later represented in the Talmud and Midrash). How sharply, though, was it a departure from the life of the community as a whole? How *revolutionary* was Jesus' attitude? Certainly, most feminists assume it to have been so, 'revolutionary', sometimes, in a quite specific modern sense. The fact that there is no explicit teaching on the matter in the gospels proves only that none was recorded; and, of course, in Marxist-inspired theology, theory is not all: as René Laurentin puts it, 'no explicit formulation of this revolution is found in the words of Christ which have been handed down to us. But this revolution is attested by his attitudes, his *praxis*, and the very characteristics of the kingdom which he founded . . .'[67] And the lack of recorded teaching has a clear explanation, as another writer puts it: 'Men made history . . . and the Bible hands down to us what they thought about God and about liberation through Jesus. In this history of masculine activity, women get a very raw deal . . .'[68]

From what *is* recorded, however, many feminists assume a radical feminism in Jesus himself. Women, like tax-collectors, were second-class citizens, relegated to 'the margins of society': Jesus, in this view, in a way quite shocking to his contemporaries, consorted with them publicly, accorded them equal status with men, spiritually redefined them in a revolution for relations between the sexes, which may even have contributed towards his death.[69]

How far can this revolutionary 'scenario' be sustained, in the light of what we know about Jesus' Palestinian environment and in the light of the gospel texts themselves? The evidence seems to indicate the need for more caution than is often shown. Certainly, Jesus' practice of speaking with women and being in their company shows an attitude to them quite different from that of the scribe-rabbis of his day. Whether the customs described in the Talmudic writings were the normal Jewish practice at this time, however, may be questioned on the evidence of the gospels themselves, if for no other reason. Women are portrayed as approaching Jesus without the kind of hesitation we would expect if Talmudic inhibitions had been generally observed; furthermore Jesus' relaxed attitude to women seems to have caused no controversy, and the gospel writers (who do not hesitate to record his conflicts with Jewish law and custom) appear to think his behaviour quite normal. There is one exception, the conversation with the Samaritan woman at the well (John 4.27): here, the disciples' surprise is caused by the fact that they are alone together (not that they are conversing) and indicates that this was, in fact, unusual behaviour on Jesus' part. In general, however, as one writer puts it, 'the evidence suggests that Jesus' normal behaviour with women was not understood to be revolutionary by people in his environment'.[70] Nor, despite Jesus' affection and respect for women, is there any evidence that he taught that the distinctive roles of the sexes in society or in the community of faith are to be broken down, though they may be differently understood. Men and women are to be initiated into the community in the same way: baptism, from the beginning, is for all without distinction. But despite Jesus' lack of inhibitions about being seen in women's company; despite the clear evidence of his willingness to confront Jewish practice and tradition without fear at any point when it was necessary to do so in the interests of justice and of truth; despite the central role played by women at critical points in his ministry; *he nevertheless appoints only male apostles*.[71] The inference, surely, is clear enough. Jesus, like Paul, regards men and women as spiritually equal: and, like Paul too, he maintains the distinctiveness of their roles, and the most enduring part of his '*praxis*' is to inaugurate an ecclesial order in which this distinctiveness will be sustained through the centuries.

10

Masculine and Feminine

How *do* men and women differ? What is the origin of the clear biblical understanding that they have different roles in society and the family, an understanding present too in all societies without exception until the present time? How is this distinction perceived in Scripture? Finally, if the broad lines of this division represent not only the instinct of human culture but also the consistent teaching of scripture, if, that is to say, we may truly infer (always remembering how such perceptions may be distorted) that the difference between the sexes as traditionally understood, is in fact part of the order of creation itself, how is this understanding to be sustained and purified within the Church, against all the pressures (explicit and implicit) from a civilization whose general tendency is the eradication of all *all* human distinctiveness? These are questions which urgently require theological attention, and to which we can offer only partial and tentative answers here.

The way in which a society, or a religion, distinguishes between the spiritual identity of men and women will be clearly reflected in the way in which it divides roles between them: so much is obvious. And it is clear that this process is more easy to achieve naturally when a society's way of life is stable: there will be particular difficulties during periods of rapid change, not least because some roles become (or seem to become) less central to the way in which a society operates. This is, of course, to say nothing about the intrinsic value or *necessity* of a social role: psychiatric nurses, for instance, were less highly regarded than secret policemen and torturers in Hitler's Germany. But this is now seen as an indictment of the Nazi view of society. And when a role - intrinsically valuable or not - becomes no longer *regarded* as valuable, it will either cease to be performed with conviction, or lead to demoralization for those who see themselves as trapped within it; there will then be for them a loss of spiritual identity. This is true of sex-linked roles, and the effects here may be particularly serious (and again we need to say that when a society ceases adequately to value a role, this may indicate that that society has begun to develop in a direction which requires to be reversed). Something of the kind appears to have happened during the last two centuries to the roles traditionally performed by women. The domestic sphere has been devalued; the life of the family is seen as less crucial to its members and to society at large. It ought to be (but is not) one of the priorities for moral and pastoral theology to explore the implications of this for society, to examine its causes, and most important of all to ask whether it can conceivably be right that Christians should accept it as inevitable.

Meanwhile, it is enough to say that in all societies it is in the domestic sphere that women's particular aptitudes and instincts have been seen as especially necessary, and that the tasks and functions associated with this have not been regarded as degrading or as having less intrinsic worth than those traditionally performed by males until comparatively recent times. The portrait of the perfect wife in the book of Proverbs (31.10-31) vividly evokes an essential human archetype. She is tireless: weaving; buying food from a distance; feeding the household and giving orders to the servants; buying land and planting vines with her earnings; giving to the poor and needy; clothing her household. She is a powerful and dignified figure, in no way her husband's drudge; and the clear delineation of their spheres of action cannot be seen as implying any superiority of the public over the domestic arena:

> Her husband is known in the gates,
> when he sits among the elders of the land.
> She makes linen garments and sells them;
> she delivers girdles to the merchant.

63

Strength and dignity are her clothing
and she laughs at the time to come.
She opens her mouth with wisdom,
and the teaching of kindness is on her tongue.
She looks well to the ways of her household,
and does not eat the bread of idleness.
Her children rise up and call her blessed;
her husband, also and he praises her:
'Many women have done excellently,
but you surpass them all.'
Charm is deceitful, and beauty is vain,
but a woman who fears the LORD is to be praised.
Give her of the fruit of her hands,
and let her works praise her in the gates.

This famous passage strikingly conveys the most obvious traditional distinction between men's and women's roles. The husband constantly leaves and returns to the domestic sphere, and is the link between the home and the wider world in which his activities unfold. He is 'known in the gates'; the wife 'looks . . . to the ways of her household'. The question inevitably poses itself: are there in human beings any consistent tendencies and capacities which we can describe as 'masculine' and 'feminine', and which correspond to this division?

Despite the sustained (and sometimes unscrupulous)[72] feminist attempt to argue that there are not, there exists in fact a considerable body of evidence, which has emerged in a wide range of disciplines, indicating that this question must be answered clearly in the affirmative. Much of the descriptive literature on the question has been collated and extensively summarized by Stephen B. Clark in his massive work *Man and Woman in Christ*.[73] Clark surveys four main types of material: evidence on individual characteristics obtained by (a) descriptive and (b) experimental methods; and evidence on 'social-structural' characteristics collected from (c) cross-cultural and (d) 'group interaction' studies: this evidence, derived from work carried out in several fields, particularly in psychology, sociology and anthropology forms a broadly coherent picture.

Two major distinctions emerge at the individual level. First, and in some ways most importantly, men tend to compartmentalize aspects of their personalities, differentiating, for instance, the physical, the emotional and the intellectual; for the woman these are all inextricably part of the same reality. Men tend towards 'differentiation', women towards 'integration'. As the phenomenologist Dietrich von Hildebrand puts it, 'we find in women a unity of personality by the fact that heart, intellect and temperament are much more interwoven; whereas in men there is a specific capacity to emancipate himself with his intellect from the affective sphere.'[74] The psychoanalyst Edith Stein can be seen broadly to concur: 'the female species is characterized by the unity and wholeness of the entire psycho-somatic personality and by the harmonious development of the faculties; the male species by the perfecting of individual capacities to obtain record achievements'.[75]

The second broad distinction which we can make between men and women at the individual level is in the general orientation of their social behaviour. This distinction underlines the one we have already made. Men tend to be more 'goal-oriented', more inclined to isolate a particular prescribed end, the pursuit and achievement of which takes on an objective value. Women's social behaviour is more concerned with caring for immediate personal needs, and with the way in which people relate to each other. The psychoanalyst F. F. Buytendijk identifies these patterns (perhaps unfortunately in view of most women's ceaseless activity) by the technical terms 'work' and 'care':

> work supposes that the one who works directs himself towards a particular end, result or goal that itself lies outside the work as such . . . The world of care is a world of actual values encountered and of possible values educed and called forth by the presence and activity of the person who cares . . .[76]

These two patterns of differentiation between men and women seen as individuals are coherent with a large body of descriptive evidence from anthropology and the social sciences and with other observed individual tendencies, among which we might single out (as less obvious to the non-specialist) a general superiority in verbal ability among females from about the age of eleven;[77] after this age, they tend to surpass males in fluency, vocabulary, grammar and spelling. A complementary superiority in 'visual-spatial' ability among males begins to develop at the same age.[78] This gives men an advantage in such activities as aiming at a target and arranging objects in a two-dimensional pattern, and it may partly account for men's apparently superior sense of direction and stronger orientation towards the physical sciences. Among 'social-structural' characteristics we might single out as particularly relevant to our inquiry is the way in which males and females tend to relate within male and female 'peer groups'. Male groups tend to be larger and more hierarchical, and effective leadership roles emerge and are accepted more naturally within them. Such groups tend to be more stable than female peer groups, and to be more important to those involved in them: females tend to be more intensely oriented towards people they can care for, to the 'small care group', particularly the family.[79] We may add to this that there is some evidence that in general females prefer male to female authority,[80] though in view of the broad context of this discussion it should be added that there is clearly a prominent minority who do not.

All these distinctions represent, it hardly needs to be said, broad general tendencies, and many individuals will to a smaller or greater degree manifest abilities associated here with the opposite sex. But certain broad lines do emerge strongly, and Clark proposes a generalization which is not merely coherent with the large mass of evidence he has surveyed but seems to indicate also that the conclusions we have reached here on the evidence and teachings of Scripture, and on the general tendency of the Christian and Jewish traditions, have to do *not* with a body of doctrine and social practice designed to place humanity (or any part of it) on a Procrustean bed which distorts and dehumanizes those thus confined, but rather with a tradition profoundly sensitive to what is requisite so that men and women may reach their full potential and become (to employ a modern cant phrase) what they truly *are*. Clark summarizes his findings in this way:

The cross-cultural evidence shows that men have held the overall governing position in every known society. The data from the other sources shows that men have characteristics which suit them for this role. The male bond allows a group of men to form a cohesive nucleus for governing a large community. Male aggressiveness equips men to protect and lead the social groupings. Superior visual-spatial ability may equip men to cope with broad social structural questions. The man's differentiated personality, along with his accomplishment orientation, also harmonizes well with an overall governing role. A governor must be able to take a disciplinary perspective, to be detached, to order a situation, to move a group forward and advance its interests, to be ready to sacrifice individual needs and feelings to the common good. Thus it can be seen that the data clusters in a coherent pattern around the male governing role.

The data clusters in a parallel way around the female domestic role. The cross-cultural evidence shows that in every known society women have cared for the young children and managed the domestic sphere. The female family bond certainly equips women for this role, as does female nurturance. Women's superior verbal ability may be related to the focus on personal relationships in domestic life. Women's integrated pattern of personality, expressed in an immediate and personal response to a social environment, also fits well with the role of caring for the young and making a home.[81]

From such a perspective, as well as from that of scriptural teaching, we may now begin to approach an essential task: that of judging and desentimentalizing some of the ways in which men and women have been caricatured without losing the essential perception a particular stereotype may (though in an attenuated form) contain. We need, certainly, to shatter damaging sexual stereotypes: but we must be clear that we do so *not* in order to lose even further our knowledge of the distinctiveness of men and women. We must break the stereotypes to reveal the archetypal understanding that may lie eternally beneath, like a bronze statue hidden beneath a crude covering of painted plaster. Scripture describes and sets God's mark on the archetypes: and the archetypal understanding of human relationships we thus attain - so long as we read

Scripture whole - gives us the means constantly to sustain a whole and unperverted perception of them. Man's authority over his wife will not then be a tyranny, for he will keep always before him the words of Christ:

> You know that among the pagans their so-called rulers lord it over them, and their great men make their authority felt. This is not to happen among you. No; anyone who wants to become great among you must be your servant, and anyone who wants to be first among you must be slave to all. For the Son of Man did not come to be served but to serve, and to give his life as a ransom for many. (Matt. 20.25-8)

We need, too, to set the judgement of Scripture on the perversion of the feminine character which is the hallmark of a sentimentalized view of the domesticated woman, by drawing a sharp contrast between the biblical perception itself, and the various sub-biblical caricatures men have invented and women have accepted, particularly under the stresses and uncertainties of an industrial culture. We need to contrast the ideal wife of Proverbs with the devitalized mezzotint of the Victorian ideal (still not without its modern versions). Here it is, exemplified by the Rev. James Baldwin Brown in his book *The Home Life* (1866). The home, in this understanding, has become an escapist dream-world, and the natural separation of the spheres of action of husband and wife an almost Manichaean polarization. The husband is 'outside the citadel . . . ofttimes sorely weary and sick of the strife'. And the wife?

> . . . Shut up with the fairest and most gracious flowers that God has planted, and the angels tend - those little ones whose angels do always behold the face of their father which is in heaven; with a state to rule which is all within easy touch of your hand; with books, and flowers, and music, and all lovely things; with a heart which God has made intuitive of great truths, and capable of high resolves; with a sense fine and sensitive to all that men get hardened to, by the genial influences which play around your life . . . At home for a man, ought to mean, shut up awhile with truth, purity, dignity, goodness, and charity, zoned with a cestus of beauty, and dressed in a lustre of love.[82]

68

This is not the true 'Eternal Feminine', any more than Betty Friedan's picture of the sentimentalized modern American wife. But if we seriously put our energies into extirpating this grisly caricature of womankind and of family life by denying even the truth of which this is a sickly perversion, the hopes for our civilization of restoring family life and a sane relationship between the sexes will become remote indeed. Rather, we need to confront the realities of a depersonalized and public civilization in which masculine aptitudes have become rampantly dominant by reasserting the importance of the domestic sphere, and of the specifically feminine aptitudes and vocation on which its life rests. Modern industrial culture is one in which the male (with his generally greater aggression, 'goal orientation', 'visual-spatial ability', and all the rest of the abilities and tendencies thus inelegantly but objectively described in the scientific literature) is peculiarly suited. But this can in the end be no more a satisfaction to him than to the woman, thus exiled, like Ruth amid the alien corn, in a world impervious to her special gifts. For the 'masculine' and the 'feminine' cannot remain authentically so, apart from each other. In the end, these are not simply objective descriptive terms; far more vitally they are principles of *relationship*; and the descriptive literature we have very briefly summarized here indicates masculine and feminine tendencies and aptitudes which, unfulfilled by those which complement them, become sterile and potentially dangerous.

Man, collectively and not individually, is in the image of God: 'and God created Man [the species] in his own image . . .; male and female created he them.' (Gen. 1.27) He created them his image so that they would be born with an instinct for loving relationship; less than themselves alone, completed only by that which is radically distinct, but also radically of the same nature. It is almost the paradox of the Trinity itself; in the words of the Orthodox theologian Paul Evdokimov:

A God with only one hypostasis (or Person) would not be Love. And if man were an isolated, solitary creature he would not be the 'image' of God. From the very outset God therefore said 'it is not good for man to be alone', and God created the human couple, as an ecclesial community. Man alone would only have been able to find the centre of his being within himself, by making the whole universe turn around his own ego.[83]

In many ways, the tragedy of the technological culture we have created is that this is precisely what has now happened. A masculine view of society, excluding the feminine values so vital to maintaining a whole and balanced civilization, has come to predominate in an industrial and scientific dispensation. And we urgently need to safeguard and foster within the Church, and to recover for society as a whole, a clear perception of men as men and women as women. We need to begin by discovering anew the special vocation of women, the knowledge that if, as Evdokimov goes on to say, 'men are *ecstatic* beings who express themselves in the world through instruments and acts', then women

> . . . are *enstatic*, they live not by acting but by *being*, they are turned towards the depths of their own nature, like the Virgin who kept the angel's words in her heart; they are present in the world by giving themselves completely. Left to himself man loses himself in abstraction and objectifications; when degraded he becomes degrading and invents a dehumanized world. The vocation of every woman is to protect the world and men like a mother, as the new Eve, and to protect and purify life as the Virgin. Women must reconvert men to their essential function, which is priesthood; the function of the spirit is to penetrate the elements of this world sacramentally and to sanctify them, to purify through prayer the work of the scientist, and to show that matter is the expression of the spirit.[84]

NOTES TO PART TWO

1 J. Winocour (ed.), *The Story of the Titanic* (London 1960), p. 296.
2 ibid., p. 172.
3 Rt Rev. Michael Marshall, in conversation with the author.
4 Una Kroll, *Flesh of my Flesh* (London 1975), p. 61.
5 ibid.
6 ibid., p. 65.
7 BBC TV Broadcast, January 1979, quoted by Margaret Stacey and Marion Price, *Women, Power and Politics* (London 1981), p. 182.

8   ibid.

9   ibid.

10 Kate Millett, *Sexual Politics* (London 1977), p. 363.

11 Kroll, op. cit., pp. 81-2.

12 Mary Daly, *Beyond God the Father* (Boston 1973), p. 26.

13 J. Mitchell, *Woman's Estate* (London 1976), p. 387.

14 Stacey and Price, op. cit., pp. 45ff.

15 June Singer, *Androgyny* (London 1977), pp. 333, 334.

16 ibid., p. 334

17 Hence, the EOC library in Manchester contains 'non-sexist' children's story books, and the EOC has from its earliest days been concerned to campaign for the removal of any distinctiveness between the education of boys and girls, in the name of 'equality'. See, for instance, Lady Howe's speech on the Erith school speech day, *EOC News*, July 1978, p. 6.

18 Mary Daly, *Gyn/Ecology* (London 1979), p. xi.

19 See e.g. K. Millett, *Sexual Politics* (London 1969), pp. 36-9.

20 B. Friedan, *It Changed My Life* (London 1977), pp. 121, 125.

21 O. Banks, *Faces of Feminism* (Oxford 1981), p. 237.

22 Rosemary Ruether, *New Woman/New Earth* (New York 1975), p. xii.

23 Eva Figes, *Patriarchal Attitudes* (London 1978), p. 14.

24 Millett, op. cit., p. 35.

25 Joanna B. Rohrbaugh, *Women: Psychology's Puzzle* (London 1981), pp. 8-9.

26 Figes, op. cit., p. 14.

27 Rohrbaugh, op. cit., p. 17.

28 Cited by Figes, op. cit., p. 14.

29 Rohrbaugh, op. cit., p. 16.

30 Figes, op. cit., p. 14.

31 Cited by P. Glick in 'The Attack on and Defence of Margaret Mead', *Royal Anthropological Institute News* (October 1983), p. 13.

32 Margaret Mead, *Male and Female* (New York 1949), pp. 31, 197.

33 Betty Friedan, *The Feminine Mystique* (London 1963), pp. 122ff.

34 Mead, op. cit., p. 40.

35 See Ruether, op. cit., pp. 3ff, who denies the historicity of 'full-blown' theories of primitive matriarchy, but nevertheless believes in a 'descent of woman' theory, in which the Hebrew tradition (see pp. 44-5 below) plays a major part.

36 P. Van den Berge, *Age and Sex in Human Societies* (Belmont 1973), p. 53; Stephen B. Clark, *Man and Woman in Christ* (Ann Arbor 1980), p. 415.

37 Susan Dowell and Linda Hurcombe, *Dispossessed Daughters of Eve* (London 1981), p. 32.

38 Dowell and Hurcombe, ibid.

39 Ruether, op. cit., pp. 15-16.

40 ibid., p. 16.

41 Dowell and Hurcombe, op. cit., p. 32.

42 Yehezkel Kaufmann, *The Religion of Israel* (London 1961), p. 103.

43 *Behind the Veil*, 'Credo' programme 2, London Weekend Television, 21 February 1982.

44 Raphael Loewe, *The Position of Women in Judaism* (London 1966), p. 48.

45 See L. Bouyer, *Mystère et Ministère de la Femme* (Paris 1976), pp. 17-18.

46 Jonathan Webber, 'Between Law and Custom: Women's Experience of Judaism', from P. Holder (ed.), *Women's Religious Experience* (London 1983), p. 149.

47 ibid., pp. 148-9.

48 Loewe, op. cit., p. 43.

49 S. Singer, *Authorised Daily Prayer Book*, p. 5.

50 Moshe Meiselmann, *Jewish Woman in Jewish Law* (New York 1978), p. 43.

51 ibid., p. 44.

52 Rabbi Samson R. Hirsch, *Commentary to Leviticus* (New York 1971), 21:43.

53 Webber, op. cit., p. 148.

54 Karl Barth, K., *Church Dogmatics* III (Edinburgh 1961), p. 156.

55 Graham Leonard, *God Alive* (London 1981), p. 40.

56 Roger Beckwith, 'The Bearing of Holy Scripture', in P. Moore (ed.), *Man, Woman and Priesthood* (London 1978), pp. 59-60.

57 ibid., p. 60.

58 Book of Common Prayer, 1662, Order for the Solemnization of Matrimony.

59 op. cit., p. 72.

60 Elisabeth Fiorenza, *In Memory of Her* (London 1983), pp. 208-9.

61 Robert Hamerton-Kelly, *God the Father* (Philadelphia 1979), p. 63.

62 Constance Parvey, 'Women in the New Testament', in Rosemary Ruether (ed.), *Religion and Sexism* (New York 1974), p. 123.

63 ibid., pp. 127-8.

64 Beckwith, op. cit., pp. 50-1.

65 Susanna Herzel (ed.), *A Voice for Women* (Geneva 1981), p. 165. (Correspondence between Henrietta Visser 't Hooft and Karl Barth)

66   See Clark, op. cit., pp. 241ff.

67   See René Laurentin, 'Jesus and Women: an Underestimated Revolution', in *Concilium* 134 (Edinburgh 1980), p. 88.

68   E. Moltmann Wendel, *The Women around Jesus* (London 1982), p. 4.

69   Hamerton-Kelly, op. cit., pp. 60-61.

70   Clark, op. cit., p. 245. My argument here closely follows Clark's.

71   This fact has led some feminists to attempt a 'reconstruction' of the New Testament record, notably Fiorenza in *In Memory of Her* (London 1983). See pp. 141-6 below.

72   For a blatant misrepresentation of the facts see for example, C. Parvey, *The Community of Women and Men in the Church: The Sheffield Report*, p. 108 (anonymous consultant on male aggression). For evidence to the contrary, see pp. 64-7 below. See also Clark, op. cit., pp. 241ff on 'feminist social science'.

73   Clark, op. cit., Chapters 16 and 17, pp. 371-467, to which pp. 64-7 below are heavily indebted.

74   Dietrich von Hildebrand, *Man and Woman* (Chicago 1965), p. 13.

75   Edith Stein, *The Writings of Edith Stein* (London 1956), p. 142.

76   F. F. Buytendijk, *Woman, a Contemporary View* (New York 1978), pp. 310-14.

77   Clark, op. cit., p. 399.

78   ibid.

79   ibid., p. 424.

80   ibid., p. 426.

81   ibid., pp. 438-9.

82   James Baldwin Brown, *The Home Life* (London 1866), pp. 19-20.

83   Paul Evdokimov, 'Ecclesia Domestica', in *A Voice for Women* (Geneva 1981), p. 176.

84   ibid., p. 283.

PART THREE

God the Father, God the Son

He was praying in a certain place, and when he ceased, one of his disciples said to him, 'Lord, teach us to pray, as John taught his disciples.' And he said to them, 'when you pray, say: "Father, hallowed be thy name . . .".' **Luke 11.1ff**

'It is hardly possible', writes Catharina Halkes, 'to call to mind a single feminist theologian, whatever her phase of development may be, who does not find the image of the Father-God a challenge and a direct confrontation.'[1] The reason why this should be so is clear enough, and Halkes goes on (almost inevitably) to quote Mary Daly's famous battle-cry, which explains, more succinctly than anything else could, why this uneasiness, even hostility, towards the biblical theme of the Fatherhood of God should be so consistently voiced by Christian feminists. 'If God is male', proclaims Daly, 'then the male is God'.[2] To see God as a Father, that is to say, has confirmed the status quo of 'patriarchal' society, and has sacralized the domination of women by men. This domination is reinforced, in this view, by the maleness of the Son, who himself constantly addresses God as Father, and who, in the dominant Christian tradition, has been represented by an exclusively male priesthood. But the 'maleness' of this 'image' of God does not merely *legitimate* human society's 'patriarchal domination' of the female sex: the Fatherhood of God is, in fact, a *product* of this domination, 'spawned', says Daly, 'in the human imagination':

> If God in 'his' heaven is a father ruling 'his' people, then it is in the 'nature' of things and according to divine plan and the order of the universe that society be male dominated . . . What is happening, of course, is the familiar mechanism by which the images and values of a given society are projected into a realm of beliefs, which in turn justify the social infrastructure. The belief system becomes hardened and objectified, seeming to have an unchangeable independent existence and validity of its own.[3]

Certain objections to this line of argument immediately present themselves. Most obviously, perhaps, it is far from clear that matriarchal religions, or religions with a mixed pantheon of gods and goddesses, were generally reflected by a higher position for women in society; there is, in fact, considerable evidence to the contrary. Certainly, matriarchal religions were never mirrored by matriarchal societies (societies, that is, ruled by a female governing caste),[4] and there is no evidence that any such society has ever existed: myths to this effect are not regarded as being historically reliable tradition by anthropologists.[5] The societies which worshipped fertility goddesses were, in fact, in the modern feminist sense, just as 'patriarchal' as the Hebrew society by which some of them were replaced, and a society regarded in some versions of the reconstructed feminist history of mankind (or 'herstory') as an archetypal destroyer of 'maternal power'.[6]

A more straightforward objection, perhaps, is the lack of evidence that, either now or in Christian history, women in any significant numbers have felt themselves excluded and oppressed by the perception of God as a Father, or have expected their own femaleness to be mirrored in their understanding of God as an object of worship. Partly, perhaps, this is because until recent times (and for most men and women even now) God has been perceived as a being who, however intimately he may have touched the lives of individuals, remains independent of and beyond ourselves. He is One whose ways are not our ways, nor are his thoughts our thoughts. We are to grow towards him, by prayer and through our struggling attempts at holiness of life; and his spirit is within us, the God within helping us to pray to the God beyond. But he in no way *reflects* our nature, nor does the life of prayer in the Christian tradition aim at the consolidation of our nature as it actually *is*. 'Becoming what you are', properly understood, involves a process of radical spiritual change and continued growth towards the authentic selfhood from which we are estranged by our own sinfulness. It means embarking on a lifelong journey of discovery towards a God who is both dynamic and unchanging, and of whose nature - even though it is infinitely beyond our understanding - we can nevertheless know something through his own self-revelation as it is recorded in holy Scripture.

11

The Revolt against God the Father

This idea of God, whether or not in the end we continue to assert its viability, is clearly one which involves some problems for an age such as ours. Whether these problems ought to involve us, not in any fundamental reassessment of our idea of God, but rather in a critical scrutiny of a culture which fails to find any necessary contact with him, may be worth considering. If an ecological disaster in some distant but civilized country led to the children of one generation being born without sexual instincts, we would not be impressed if when fully grown the cleverer ones, having been imprisoned in remote academies, began to write books describing the institution of marriage in particular, and sexuality in general, as belonging to a more primitive stage of our development. It may, in other words, be our society which needs to reassess itself, rather than our idea of God which needs to be recast, if God and modern culture are to re-establish contact. This having been said, it is certainly necessary to add that, though God may be infinite and unchanging, human ideas about him - though in one way constant - have always changed in their expression, to meet constantly changing historical needs and modes of thought and that *this* kind of exploration is often necessary if old theologies are not gradually to lose touch with the God they seek to apprehend and inadequately, though objectively, convey. And there may be a point at which the more adventurous among those trying to rediscover God among the debris of decaying cultural expression will appear to have gone beyond legitimate bounds, even to be dismantling the faith, when in fact they are returning to its true basis. The difficulty is that there is also the possibility that they may have done in fact what they seem to the less adventurous to have done, that is, abandoned the faith itself; there is also the possibility that what *appears* to be a dead and oppressive formula may, to one who has opened himself to its meaning, be no mere formula at all, but an indispensable gateway to spiritual knowledge and freedom.

How are we to chart our course in these uncertain waters?

How are we, in particular, to assess the feminist revolt against the Christian tradition's deeply rooted symbolic perception of God as being our Father? It is important to understand that, however powerful the influence of secular feminism over the Christian women's movement may be, at *this* point, Christian feminists are engaged at a level which can only be described as 'spiritual' or 'religious'. And though there is no lack of consequent theological speculation about how Jesus' approach to God in prayer, 'Abba, Father', is to be replaced or otherwise dealt with, it is not at the speculative level that the difficulty tends to be most vividly discerned, nor is it in such terms that it is expressed with the greatest conviction.

How are we to understand the problem? An instructive case-history here, perhaps, is that of the artist and feminist mystical writer, Meinrad Craighead, for fourteen years a Roman Catholic Benedictine nun. Craighead recalls what she believes to be her first mystical experience of God. At the age of about seven, she was sitting in the shade outside her grandparents' clapboard house in Little Rock, Arkansas. She sat stroking her dog, holding its head. The dog held her gaze. As she looked into its eyes, she realized that

> I would never travel further than into this animal's eyes. They were as deep, as bewildering, as unattainable as a night sky. Just as mysterious was a clear awareness of water within me, the sound in my ears, yet resounding from my breast. I gazed into the dog's eyes and listened to the sound of rushing water inside me. I understood 'This is who God is. My Mother is water and she is inside me and I am in the water.'[7]

It was a moment which was to determine 'a life-time preoccupation with and persistence toward the source'. But although Craighead's 'irrevocable orientation to the primordial matrix' was now established, it still lacked form. Soon afterwards she discovered that form: in a Roman Catholic elementary school in Chicago, she stumbled across a photograph of the bulbous and faceless fertility goddess, the Venus of Willendorf. 'The recognition was immediate and certain', she recalls; 'I knew that this was she whom I had heard in the water and beyond the dog's eyes.'[8] From this time onwards her spiritual course was set: 'being with her', she goes on 'was undoubtedly the origin of my desire for a life of contemplative prayer and to be an artist. I had then, and still have, one essential prayer: "show me your face".'⁹

What some more orthodox Christians might think a fundamental incompatibility between such a perception of God and the Christian revelation of him did not deter her from pursuing a religious vocation as a Benedictine sister. She consciously made the choice to 'reinvest' her Christian heritage rather than abandoning it, the 'negative patriarchal values' of Christianity, implicit in 'the orthodox image of the transcendent Father God' being balanced and 'enriched'¹⁰ by her personal, and strictly private, vision. But the vision remained, for her, the primary revelation: 'through half a lifetime of Christian worship', she confesses, 'my secret worship of God the Mother has been the sure ground of my spirituality.'¹¹

The life of a Benedictine religious was not, it might be thought, ideal for the nurture of such a spirituality. During the fourteen years, her disillusionment grew as was, surely, inevitable: 'the community mind', she complains, 'sought the survival of a social and spiritual tradition. I thought monastic life was about spiritual freedom and the risks of an unorthodox life.' The other sisters were 'dependent, inauthentic people estranged from themselves', unimaginative and with few 'experiential resources'. In the end, as she relates, 'my own spiritual orientation and creative work became so opposed to the communal heteronomy and the worship of an exalted masculine god-image that it was necessary for me to leave'.¹²

This is the personal experience of an unusual woman; nevertheless, after all the necessary cautions on premature generalizations have been registered, we can still see this 'herstory' as a kind of *locus classicus* of feminist spirituality. Some Christian feminists would not go so far as Craighead does in identifying the divine with an exalted *feminine* god-image. Few, nevertheless, would actually argue with any conviction against doing so and most would defend such an orientation, including some of those who, like Sarah Maitland, retain alongside their feminist vision an openness to a more

orthodox spirituality, and even some clearly perceptible
hankerings after an orthodox theology. Craighead's story
vividly represents certain key themes. We can note the refusal
to accept in any way the divine inspiration of Scripture, a
refusal implicit in her description of the God of the Bible as 'an
exalted masculine god-image'; we could almost add Daly's
words 'spawned in the human imagination'. This is paralleled
by the scant respect accorded to what one would have supposed
a normal aspiration of any monastic establishment, 'the
survival of a social and spiritual tradition'. Underlying both
these refusals is her rejection of what she describes here as
'communal heteronomy' (we might translate this as 'the
demands of a disciplined community life'), and her complementary assertion of the primacy of her personal autonomy,
of her 'own spiritual orientation'.

It is clear that this is more than the classic story of the
imaginative young woman who plunges into the religious life
without any clear idea of what it involves, and then discovers
the hard way that she has no vocation to it. Craighead does not
merely *withdraw* from monastic life: at the same time she (and
not merely for herself) rejects what it is that makes the religious
life possible: a shared attitude to the faith, and to the rule by
which, in community, the faith is lived out. Over against this,
she erects a completely private, even 'secret', spiritual life; one
with an entirely personal origin, and which has no point of
contact with the tradition with which she nevertheless remains
uneasily affiliated. She accepts, still, 'the Christian mysteries',
but on her own terms; terms which themselves undermine the
basis of her acceptance. In its autonomy, her spirituality
negates the very nature of Christian prayer, which is that it is
always a participation in the prayer of the *whole* Church, in this
world and the next. Even when he prays alone, the Christian
must always be part of the Church; personal prayer is never
private prayer, let alone 'secret' prayer, prayer which must be
kept hidden from the community.

It is this insistence on spiritual independence thus understood
(with its implicit refusal of community) which as much as
anything indicates the character of Christian feminism. The
existence of groups of like-minded women who meet for 'non-

sexist' discussion and worship in no way invalidates this suggestion. Christian community is essentially the unity of the diverse and the various; it is, in Paul's indispensable analogy, like the community of the different parts of the human body. The selective community of the identically defined, who have made the basis of selection the willingness of the members of the group to underline their existing personality and to share their existing views, may have usefulness in certain limited situations such as the operation of a pressure group or a political party. But it can never be the basis of Christian community, membership of which will always involve at some point the submerging of an individuality (which nevertheless remains intact) in the whole. It involves, quite simply, the surrender - not the assertion - of personal autonomy: the Christian is incorporated into Christ as a member of his body, distinct but not independent. The Christian community is, in fact, *essentially* a 'heteronomy'; and although it is possible to say, in a certain technical sense, that an excessive tendency to 'dependence' (perceived as a psychological problem) may be associated with immaturity and a lack of willingness to take spiritual risks, it is also necessary to insist that *dependence*, properly understood, must be seen as one indispensable sign of an authentically Christian spirituality; we are, none of us, independent of God, and entirely depend on him for each second of our continued existence: and the continuing knowledge of this must be a constant element in any sustained and growing relationship with him.

The psychological difficulties of this attitude to faith, for the 'feminist consciousness', are clear enough. We have already seen how, in different ways, the various strains of secular feminism are based on the quest for freedom from dependence. In the first place, this means dependence on the male sex; and we can see that in this context 'dependence' often means 'interdependence', since the woman's rejection of her own dependence will also, where it is recognized, involve a rejection of the man's complementary dependence - emotional and otherwise - on her. Broadly speaking, this shows itself in two ways. Some feminists look towards an androgynous society, in which males and females would be independent of the opposite sex for emotional completion: the new androgynous personality which would in such a society develop for both sexes would already contain within itself both masculine and feminine; thus women would be freed from the shackles of 'complementarity'. Others, as we have seen, have asserted a full separatist and matriarchalist feminism, in which male 'domination' is by-passed or even in theory reversed, by asserting female values within a feminist alternative society. Sometimes, these two attitudes can be observed co-existing uneasily. For both Carol Christ and Naomi Goldenberg, for instance, the symbol of the Mother-Goddess helps women understand their nurturant maternal nature as a vital and central part of women's experience: and yet it is also permissible, even desirable, for a woman actually to refuse to care for her child as a step towards her liberation from the tyranny of 'sexually determined roles'. 'Maternal nature', here, becomes a kind of consumer option, an experience to be tasted, rather than a vocation requiring persistence and dedication.[13]

Again, rejection of the fatherhood of God can be seen as part of a general rejection of 'authoritarianism', and for Dr Christ the worship of the Goddess has the effect of minimizing the 'hierarchalism' characteristic of all traditional religions. For both Christ and Goldenberg, indeed, male spirituality is essentially hierarchical, and female spirituality essentially egalitarian. And yet Carol Christ can also make claims that the 'overarching divine principle' is better expressed in female terms, and Goldenberg asserts that any male involved in the Goddess cult cannot be regarded as an equal.[14] This last conclusion is, of course, an entirely logical outcome of other assumptions, and we are forced in fairness to the provisional conclusion that the symbol of the Goddess is not a promising foundation for a feminist theology of any stability or per-suasiveness, and that it would not at this stage be entirely justified to assume from the examples so far quoted that this symbol has a consistent attraction for the Christian women's movement. Even so, it is worth while at the same time to recall the opinion of a feminist thinker as substantial and as influential as Rosemary Ruether, writing of the section of the Goddess movement represented by feminist 'Wicca' (or witchcraft), that 'it is possible that we are witnessing in this movement the first stirrings of what may become a new stage of human religious consciousness'.[15]

The essential common factor between this and feminist theologies which are, superficially at least, more 'orthodox', is the insistence on liberation from the masculine principle in creation, and the declaration of women's sexual independence. Thus, Sara Maitland, one of those feminists within the Catholic tradition who still assert the central importance of the Blessed Virgin Mary in the economy of salvation, can integrate her into the feminist vision by claiming the feast of the Annunciation as a celebration of 'women's autonomous sexuality': the virgin birth, having been acomplished without biological male participation, thus becomes a symbolic triumph for the feminist dream.[16]

12

The 'Problem' of God

The quest for a 'non-hierarchical' doctrine of God which no longer implies a relationship between creator and creature of authority and obedience is, it should be noted at this stage, not one which is confined to feminists alone. Nor are the theological 'problems' posed in western culture by the Father God of Christian tradition new ones. One feminist commentator, writing in 1980, could even deride the preoccupation of the Christian women's movement with the rebellion against God the Father by asserting baldly that

This God . . . has been dead and quite irrelevant for some time now. In intellectual circles (ecclesiastic and academic) he has never really recovered from his encounter with the radical skepticism and secular science of several centuries ago. What of him lingered to be mocked by Kierkegaard and dismissed by Nietzsche is now regarded with a deep indifference, and the theist/atheist debate itself has become in our culture intellectually marginal. The prerequisite to our executing this god is not raising feminist consciousness, but erecting a straw man.[17]

Certainly, whether or not we are prepared to defend the relevance of the traditional ways of describing God, it would be idle to deny the difficulties for an age such as ours of the notion of a transcendent creator God, with whom we have something like a personal relationship, and who is active in the lives of men and women, sometimes intervening directly at critical points in human affairs. And without doubt, the word 'God' itself no longer has the instinctively and generally accepted significance that once it did, and from this fact emerges an unavoidable question: does this mean that the expression 'God' no longer *has* a meaning, and that we have to discover one *de novo?* Does it mean, as Professor John Macquarrie puts the question, 'that we must be prepared for just as revolutionary a development in our conception of God as took place when the old mythological ideas of God were discredited and then superseded by subtler conceptions?'[18] Just as the God of the Bible displaced earlier and cruder notions of divinity, do we now need, for a human race 'come of age', a post-biblical way of approaching God?

The problems of traditional ideas of God are by no means purely philosophical ones: they are also political and sociological. Undoubtedly, the intellectual revolution of the last three centuries has made it difficult to think of God's authority in exactly the way that we did; but the social and political upheavals of the twentieth century have made it hard for many to think of *any* authority in a positive way. The German feminist theologian Dorothée Sölle tells us that she conceived her own objections to 'the divine super-power' in Auschwitz;[19] and though we may say that there is an obvious difference between the loving and sacrificial authority of God and the demonic authority of a Hitler or a Stalin, this archetypal twentieth-century experience undoubtedly tells us a great deal about the *psychology* of much post-war theological speculation. Sölle's question, forty years afterwards, is still not one to elicit any glib or easy response. The question is

. . . whether obedience is not precisely one of those ideas which are no longer valid after the holocaust. The question how deeply the conditioning of the Christian mind to an attitude of total obedience prepared the ground for Nazism is a matter for historians. For theologians the fact that Eichmann, who was enrolled in the German YMCA by his parents, constantly stressed obedience as did Rudolf Hösz whose father destined him for the priesthood, should be enough to rob this concept of all its theological innocence. Nor does it help to make a distinction between the 'true' or 'proper' obedience towards *God* and obedience to *man*. Can one want and develop an attitude towards God which one criticizes in people in their attitude towards men and human institutions?[20]

These are questions to which we must return. At this point, though, it is enough to identify an often guilt-ridden pre-occupation with searching for the roots of tyranny within Christian theology and practice as being, understandably (though not always defensibly), one of the recurring themes of much post-war theological writing; and to place feminist theology within this general context.

The scientific and philosophical revolution of recent centuries, together with more recent developments have, then, for some writers at any rate, combined to give a certain urgency to the problem of how we are to describe God and to think about him; and feminist disquiet must in fairness be seen as part of a more general questioning. We have seen one feminist answer to the problem: to replace the allegedly 'authoritarian' symbol of God as a Father, and to think of him instead as 'Mother'. Another solution, at first sight less drastic, is to 'balance' our idea of God by such liturgical formulae as 'in the name of the Father and the Mother, the Son and the Spirit',[21] the difficulties of which are equally great: are we discussing an enlargement of the Trinity? Or a Trinitarian God one of whose persons is now seen as a kind of androgynous 'parent', 'God the Mother/ Father'? Serious feminist theologians are by no means oblivious to such problems, and a more promising feminist approach, perhaps, certainly one less open to ridicule, is to adopt a policy which depersonalizes God altogether, avoiding entirely a symbolism which refers to the relationships of the human family. Thus, Sölle suggests images taken from the language of the mystics: 'source of all that is good', 'life-giving wind', 'water of life', 'light'; all expressions devoid of any human reference and therefore of any potentially authoritarian content.[22] In the mystical tradition, she suggests, the emphasis is not on obedience to God, but on union with him: and this emphasis enables our relationship with God to become one of 'agreement and consent' (note the curious return to personal symbolism), and this can then become the nature of religion: 'when this happens', concludes Sölle, 'solidarity will replace obedience as the dominant virtue.'[23]

The choice proposed by writers like Sölle is, we may say, one between two types of religion which are, in the end, understood as mutually exclusive. The two types are distinguished by the secular humanist writer Erich Fromm as 'humanitarian' and 'authoritarian'.[24] 'Authoritarian' religion emphasizes obedience; 'humanitarian' religion, in sharp distinction, has as its aim and chief virtue 'self-realization'; in such a religion, as Sölle puts it, 'resistance to growth is the cardinal sin'.[25] Whether, in fact, this distinction is helpful, or accurately observed, or inclusive of all available types of religion is a question that naturally poses itself, and it will be necessary in due course to ask whether obedience to God and human self-realization are truly contradictory goals within the Christian dispensation. Meanwhile, it is enough to note once more the clear, almost dualistic opposition between them for religious feminists. For the feminist consciousness, self-realization, by definition, is attained on one's own terms; and 'being one with the whole' has as its starting-point and origin one's own personal spiritual experience. 'God' and 'self-realization' may then, within this general framework of assumptions, become almost synonymous.

No one has developed this aspect of feminist religious thought more forcefully than the highly influential 'post-Christian' theologian, Mary Daly. Daly's theology of God begins from her understanding of women as 'marginal beings who have no stake in a sexist world'.[26] As such, Daly claims, they have 'access to the knowledge that neither the Father, nor the son, nor the Mother *is* God'. Anthropomorphic symbols for God, constructed by human imagination, fail to convey that

God is 'Be-ing'. Daly hyphenates this word, both to distance herself from earlier interpretations of it, and to emphasize that God is not *a being*. To think of God as a person is to 'reify' him, and thus to separate him from humanity. This process is 'demonic' in some of its consequences, and women are in a unique position to perceive this:

> The dichotomizing-reifying-projecting syndrome has been charac-
> teristic of patriarchal consciousness, making 'the Other' the
> repository of the contents of the lost self. Since women are now
> beginning to recognize in ourselves the victims of such dichotomiz-
> ing processes, the insight extends to other manifestations of the
> pathological splitting off of reality into falsely conceived
> opposites.[27]

Her solution is to conceive of God not as a noun but as a verb; not, therefore, as 'a being', but as 'Be-ing' itself. By itself this is, apart from the hyphen, familiar enough. For Daly, though, it becomes as much a statement about the condition of women as one about the nature of God. 'Hasn't the naming of "God" as a noun', she asks,

> . . . been an act of murdering that dynamic Verb? and isn't the Verb
> infinitely more personal than a mere static noun? The anthro-
> pomorphic symbols for God may be intended to convey personality,
> but they fail to convey that God is Be-ing. Women who are
> experiencing the shock of non-being and the surge of self-
> affirmation against this are inclined to perceive transcendence as
> the Verb in which we participate - live, move, and have our being.[28]

God perceived as Being is not, of course Mary Daly's invention, and her thinking here, despite the obvious contrasts between the two, shows the clear influence of Paul Tillich, who is an influence not only on Daly but on other feminist theologians.[29] Tillich, too, rejects what Daly calls the 'reifying' of God: that which is ultimate must be something in which man participates, from which he is not cut off by seeing God as a separate entity. God is being itself, 'the power of being', or 'the ground of being': he is not a particular being. The appeal of this kind of thinking to feminist theologians is clear enough, and Tillich himself sees its importance as one way of talking about

God which transcends 'the alternative male-female', and which is 'capable of being developed over against a one-sided male-determined symbolism'.[30] Tillich, however, understands the necessity for establishing a conception of God purged of masculine overtones not as one equally pressing for all Christians, but as being particularly important for Protestant theology. And this priority has clear historical reasons:

> The symbolic power of the image of the Holy Virgin from the fifth century after Christ up to our time raises a question for Protestantism, which has radically removed this symbol in the struggle of the Reformation against all human mediators between God and man. In this purge the female element in the symbolic expression of ultimate concern was largely eliminated. The spirit of Judaism with its exclusively male symbolism prevailed in the Reformation. Without doubt, this was one of the reasons for the great successes of the Counter Reformation over against the originally victorious Reformation. It gave rise within Protestantism itself to the often rather effeminate pictures of Jesus in Pietism; it is the cause of many conversions to the Greek or Roman Churches, and it is also responsible for the attraction of Oriental mysticism for many Protestant humanists.[31]

But for Protestantism, says Tillich, the reinstatement of the symbol of the Holy Virgin cannot now be achieved: concrete religious symbols cannot be re-established once they are destroyed. Having reached this point, we can only proceed now by moving beyond the Trinitarian conception of God. God as 'ground of being', Tillich continues, 'points to the mother-quality of giving birth, carrying and embracing and, at the same time, of calling back . . .'[32]

God as being is no recent development, though its use in Christian theology *over against* the Trinitarian and other biblical conceptions of God certainly is; and earlier speculation on this theme can be seen for obvious reasons to proceed in very different ways. For St Thomas Aquinas and the high Middle Ages, God was seen as 'Being-itself' (*ipsum esse*). Since, being God, he has no unrealized potentiality, he is therefore changeless and unchangeable, in contrast with his creation, which must change to realize its potential. This parallels the contrast in earlier Greek philosophy between 'being' and 'becoming': *being* cannot change since it is perfect; the world nevertheless does, observably, change: and therefore contains degrees of being or perfection. For Aristotle change, or *becoming*, is the process of realizing potentiality. The relevance of this distinction to the feminist movement is not at first apparent, nor on the face of it does it contain any sexist bias requiring urgent attention today. For Mary Daly, though, it is not (as one might have predicted) a quaint relic of a defunct philosophy, but a living force in modern civilization: the 'split' between being and becoming is part of 'the dichotomizing propensities in our culture',[33] of which the distinction perceived by society between masculine and feminine is also a sign. These propensities require to be overcome, and for the Mary Daly of *Beyond God the Father*, 'androgynous wholeness is the essential healing we seek': 'we might consider', she suggests,

> . . . the probability that if the male intellectual élite has been fixated upon a split between becoming and being, this in all likelihood reflects the situation of the élite, who benefit from a static, hierarchical cultural climate and who would be threatened by total openness to the future. 'Becoming' then becomes domesticated under the reign of reified 'being', which can present 'things as they are' to the consciousness of the privileged who want it that way. It would not serve such interests if 'becoming' were to blow off the lid of objectified 'being'.[34]

Daly has, in fact, paradoxically provided here, and in a dramatic way, her own distinctively feminist solution to a problem which has always been, as Alan Richardson puts it, 'both the permanent task and the culminating problem of Christian theology as such':[35] to hold together the personal God of biblical revelation with the God of Greek philosophy. 'The problem', writes Richardson, 'may be stated thus: Being is the most abstract of all possible ideas: the God of the Bible is the most living and personal of all conceivable realities. How are the two conceptions to be held together?'[36] Daly here, ironically and with consummate ease, unites the two conceptions of God by seeing them both as oppressive, and by describing the operation of their oppressiveness in almost identical terms: both Being (as distinct from becoming) and the Father-God of Judaeo-Christian tradition represent the 'dichotomizing-reifying-projecting syndrome' which she sees as 'characteristic of "patriarchal consciousness".' Being, traditionally conceived, is now not merely philosophically *distinct* from, but is seen as *over against* 'Becoming', a word which for her is identified with a rising tide of affirmation of female consciousness. 'Human becoming' (specifically the liberation of women) and 'Be-ing' (God) have now become entirely indistinct; for Daly, as we have seen, the second coming of Christ in this mutation is replaced by 'the second coming of women'. Women's liberation is for her 'synonymous' with the Antichrist: the end of 'Patriarchy' will mean the end of 'Christolatry'.[37]

Though Mary Daly, like the fat boy in *Pickwick*, loves to make our flesh creep, we have here - once the overtones of the Hammer film are removed - a theology of God which, in its broad outlines, would probably be accepted by most feminist theologians. Whatever the idea of God - or God(ess) as Rosemary Ruether prefers - which any particular feminist theologian entertains, it is generally one which sees an 'objectified' deity as a source of injustice and alienation. Even when, as in the Goddess movement, what is apparently an 'entity' is set up, its origins in a consciously and subjectively contrived act of 'symbol' creation are usually clear, and its *purpose* is to nurture female 'becoming'. And when God is seen as 'Be-ing', or symbolized in images from the mystical tradition (cut off from their original context within a Trinitarian religious understanding) it is so that 'self-realization', understood as being over-against obedience to God, may be freed from the shackles of a biblical religious culture. One intended consequence of this replacement of obedience by 'solidarity' is that the alleged distance from humanity, and the supposed irrelevance to its concerns, of an objectively perceived (i.e. 'reified') Divinity, will be overcome.

The most obvious, and surely the most overwhelming, objection to such a theology is that for most Christian men and women it is difficult to imagine a way of approaching God more entirely incomprehensible, and therefore more distant or irrelevant. This is equally true of better-known versions of a post-biblical Deity such as Tillich's 'ground of being', and certainly of such philosophical supplements as *ipsum esse*. Their value as part of the Church's understanding of the nature of God may be argued one way or another: by themselves, they simply dissolve, in the words of Alan Richardson, 'in the shadows of pantheism, or in the obscurities of philosophical speculation'.[38]

Certainly, we need at this point to ask whether such non-personal ideas of God as Being, (a concept which despite such proof-texts as Exodus 3.14 owes its prominence to Greek philosophy) can possibly be viable for an authentically Christian theology unless they are related in some significant way to the God of the Bible, the Lord of History, whose nature is revealed in his only Son, who for us men and for our salvation came down from heaven, and was incarnate of the Virgin Mary. It is surely not possible to *pray* consistently to anything so lacking in concreteness as a 'ground of being'. And whatever Christian feminists may say, if they are truly to remain *Christian* feminists, that is to say followers of Christ, it is his conception of God which before all others is definitive for Christian prayer and ought to be definitive for Christian theology too. Here, the starting-point must be: the disciples see Jesus at prayer; they ask him 'Lord, teach us to pray'; he replies: 'when you pray, say *Father* . . .' Here is the beginning of all Christian prayer; and the particular use of the word 'Father' here as a form of address carries, it will be seen, a vital part of its meaning, which Matthew's fuller form '*Our* Father' develops, indicating both that it is within the Christian community that our prayer unfolds, and that we understand God's nature as being essentially one with which we are intended to have *relationship*. And the definitive symbol *Father* for God, which belongs if anything at all does to the domain of *revelation* rather than that of theological reflection or humanly con-structed analogy can have no meaning unless that meaning is perceived in the context of the relationship it implies. 'When used in Christian thought and speech as a term for God', wrote Karl Barth towards the end of his life, 'the word "Father" is always to be employed and understood in precisely the same sense that it has . . . in the introit to the Lord's Prayer, namely as a vocative'.[39] And when 'Father' *is* used and understood in such a way, Barth continues,

> . . . this word gives the required precision, the appropriate fulness, and the authentic interpretation to a word that in itself is indefinite, empty, and ambivalent, namely, the word 'God'. God himself, the one true and real God, obviously does not need this in order to avoid indistinctness, emptiness and ambivalence. But the word 'God' in all human languages does need it, for it can mean everything for some, this or that for others, and even nothing at all, or a mere illusion, for others . . . Christians, however, move through this misty territory invoking the Father with crying, sighing, singing, and rejoicing, praising the Father, thanking the Father, and above all praying to the Father, their life being a life in this vocative. They do not do this with the claim that of themselves they know better than everyone else . . . they know too much about the one true and real God not to be clear that authentic interpretation cannot come to the word 'God' by any human defining, meditating, or speculating - not even their own - but comes only when the Word of God aids the intrinsically impotent word 'God' and gives it the only possible and correct content.[40]

The life and theology of Karl Barth, as it happens, can be seen in several crucial ways to illuminate the present discussion. The connection between his theology of God and his view of the Pauline texts on the headship of the male in marriage and the Christian community (which we have already touched on) have not gone unnoticed by feminist writers like Mary Daly, who describes his opinions (along with those of Augustine, Aquinas, Luther and Knox) as 'crudely dehumanizing'.[41] His views, too, on the themes of authority and revelation as such (and not simply in particular contexts) run directly counter to deeply held feminist principle. It needs to be said, of course, that Barth's extreme revelationism, which entirely denies the place of any kind of natural theology, is also challenged by many non-feminist Christians, too. Few ordinary Christians, however (theologians, unhappily, are another matter), would challenge in quite the same way his assertion that Christianity is a religion given and revealed by God, and not one created by men:

Barth's positive assertions about the ultimate theological primacy of the divine Word, the *Logos*, bridge most historical divides between Christians (it is his denials of the place of human reason that many Christians would themselves deny).

His emphasis, too, on the authority of God is precisely one guaranteed to arouse feminist suspicion and resentment, even though this authority extends over all humanity, male and female alike: the fact that it is exercised by a God seen as *Father* is calculated, in this view, to achieve the subservience most particularly of the female half of the human race. But even if we do not press home this precisely feminist point, the feminist emphasis on 'solidarity' with God rather than 'obedience' to him further indicates Barthian theology as being innately and irredeemably anti-feminist. It is the 'culture of obedience' (*Gehorsamskultur*)[42] held to derive from an attitude to God such as Barth's which can - so runs the argument - be used to legitimate not only the oppression of women, but *all* human oppression, even one, in Sölle's opinion at least, as monstrous as the Nazi tyranny itself. And the associated view of a 'once for all' revelation can be represented as equally oppressive, since it rules out God's continuing activity in revealing himself through the growth of human knowledge and understanding, and the evolution of human society.

One interesting example of what we might term the theology of human self-realization is to be found in the work of the German writer Emmanuel Hirsch, to whom Barth turned his critical attention in April 1934, the same month in which he wrote the letter we have already quoted defending Pauline teaching on male headship. Sölle's formula, 'resistance to growth is the cardinal sin', might equally have been conceived by Hirsch: 'if we in theology and Church are too small . . .', he wrote, 'if we cannot, by surrendering all the prejudice stemming from the past and all our need for assurance and security risk ourselves to the inrushing "new" . . . then we are cast out'.[43] It has been, of course, a recurring theme throughout the century. Something of the same spirit was shown over thirty years later by the liberal Anglican bishop Paul J. Moore Jr, who recalls that, when he was considering whether it was right to ordain women to the priesthood, he strengthened himself with the dictum 'whenever you are faced with a difficult choice, go with the future, not the past'.[44] Against Hirsch's line, Barth rigidly inisisted on the vital need for theological orthodoxy, based on submission to God as he has revealed himself, and not on our idea of God deriving from our own understanding of human needs and human society. The object of theology is 'the Word of God, or Jesus Christ, crucified and risen', who 'stands as Lord, as Creator, as Reconciler, as Redeemer . . .' 'Before Him', continues Barth, in typically 'authoritarian' vein, 'only faith and obedience are of value'. And he goes on:

> He is indeed with us every day until the end of the world, but not in such a way that He would be swallowed up by our days and the bold grasping which is the significance of our days, not in such a way that we should have the mission and authority to interpret our days as we like, so as then to give His holy name confidently to the thing our interpretation has created. It is enough and more than enough if we with our daring, grasping and interpreting in large and small things, may walk before him in fear and joy, praying, thanking and praising, because we are accepted in grace . . .[45]

Barth, in fact, here exemplifies *par excellence* everything against which a 'humanitarian' or 'liberation' theology (feminist or not) sets its face. And it needs firmly to be said that nothing could more dramatically indicate the magnitude of the theological error committed by Sölle and by the entire school she can be seen to represent, a school whose assumptions (with or without an admixture of Marxism) bear a striking resemblance to those of Hirsch. Barth's attack on Hirsch forms, in fact, part of a general attack on the so-called 'German National Church'; and Hirsch's plea for freedom from the dead hand of the past and for openness to 'the inrushing new' is made precisely in the context of a plea for Christians to respond to the so-called 'German Hour' ushered in by Adolf Hitler, by understanding it as a 'meeting with God'.[46] And it is exactly Barth's 'authoritarian' insistence on the uprooting of heresy and on obedience to God that he holds up defiantly, like a banner, in repudiation of this peculiarly odious betrayal; an insistence he was to maintain through dismissal from his

academic post and expulsion from Germany, and which
continued to inspire those Christians within Germany who
remained to struggle against the Nazi oppression. Nor was this
in any way theologically eccentric, a kind of malfunctioning of
what one ought to have expected. Human 'self-realization' on
mankind's own terms has always been seen in mainstream
Christian tradition as a profoundly dangerous aspiration, and it
is only a theological tradition which denies or weakens the
Church's doctrine of sin and of the fall of man which could
suppose that it is anything else. And to hold up the authority of
God against man's overweening arrogance and lust is, to a
spirituality derived from an acceptance of that authority, no
mere perversity. It is, on the contrary, an almost unavoidable
impulse to draw strength from the profound and ancient
biblical theme of trust in the inseparable power and mercy of
God. Even Jesus' cry of dereliction on the cross, 'My God, my
God why hast thou forsaken me?' the opening line of
Psalm 22, can never then be final - and the psalm goes on:

> Ye that fear the Lord, praise him; all ye the seed of Jacob glorify
> him; and fear him, all ye the seed of Israel.
> For he hath not despised nor abhorred the affliction of the
> afflicted; neither hath he hid his face from him; but when he cried
> unto him, he heard. (AV)

13
Dealing with the Bible

Though in general Christian feminists are united by an attitude
to the biblical tradition itself which, to say the very least, is
considerably less than slavish, we can nevertheless distinguish
three broad approaches different enough to explain occasional
signs of mutual suspicion between their respective protagonists.
One approach, at first sight perhaps the most moderate, comes
to the text in a way which seeks to show that, though much
biblical symbolism (particularly that of the Father-God) may

appear sexist at the level of surface analogy, real textual meaning operates at a deeper level, and is essentially 'sexually inclusive'. A second approach, probably the most common, simply proposes that the Bible presents a mixed bag of 'sexist' and 'non-sexist' elements, and claims the right to draw on those parts of the biblical tradition which can be judged to be supportive of the feminist view, and to ignore those parts thought from a modern feminist standpoint to be inimical to it. This is a procedure which can be clearly distinguished from other attempts at selectivity in Christian history (such as the 'canon within the canon' of the Reformation) by the detailed and localized way in which it operates. It is (arguably) defensible to object as Luther did to the inclusion in the New Testament of the epistle of James, or like some old-fashioned biblical critics to attach more weight for most purposes to the synoptic gospels than to that of St John. The feminist approach, however, is (in effect) to work through the text verse by verse, for all the world like a censor with blue pencil in hand: this is a procedure we have already seen vividly illustrated by the methodical feminist filleting of the epistles of St Paul (an extreme implementation of this approach is actually to rewrite the text where it is deemed linguistically sexist, though this procedure has its limitations, as we shall see).

The third view is that which dismisses the entire biblical and monotheist tradition as irredeemably sexist, but which nevertheless believes in a religious dimension in life, and seeks to preserve this by creating a new mythology ('telling our stories' is an essential feminist activity) and by asserting God as 'immanent mother', a term understood as being over against 'transcendent father'.

These three approaches to Scripture correspond with more generalized feminist attitudes to the Christian tradition: first, the 'reformist' view (to use Naomi Goldenberg's description)[47] which seeks to explain the Church's alleged 'sexism' as the result of its own misunderstanding of its heritage and seeks to assuage feminist discontent by adjustments in its practices; secondly, a more radical approach, which believes in the need for sweeping readjustments in its theological and symbolic understanding of God and of the nature of humanity; thirdly, the approach epitomized by the Goddess movement, which seeks for, and according to a well-known feminist[48] within the Church may be well on the way towards achieving, a new stage in mankind's religious understanding.

This threefold typology might perhaps be conveniently remembered as being a distinction between what, for future reference I will call Grade 1, Grade 2, and Grade 3 feminism, in ascending order of openly acknowledged radicalism (this does not, of course say anything about how radical the *intentions* of any particular approach may be, or how radical its possibly unintended *effects*). This typology (though not in these terms) was proposed in its specific application to attitudes to Scripture, by Robert Hamerton-Kelly,[49] who himself epitomizes the first approach, or Grade 1: this grading would probably apply to most of the liberal bishops and male theologians who have dabbled in feminist theology, though undoubtedly some have advanced gingerly into Grade 2, and one at least has shown distinct signs of Grade 3.[50]

These boundaries are, of course, to some extent artificial, and there is a good deal of crossing backwards and forwards between the areas they delineate; furthermore, there exist more affinities between them than at first appears. All of them, for instance, assume the entire cultural contingency of a symbol such as 'Father': either it is an extension of 'patriarchal' values; or if, as is very rarely admitted, it can be seen (particularly in the mouth of Jesus) to have a meaning which is *not* oppressive, then this is a meaning which is no longer naturally available to us because we are debarred by our own cultural dependence.[51] What is *not* assumed is that any such symbol might legitimately be seen as forming part of Divine Revelation itself, for this would mean accepting that it might have the power of itself to transcend and thus stand over against culture. Thus, Hamerton-Kelly, though he sees the Father-God symbol as expressing Jesus' own deepest experience of God, nevertheless cannot bring himself to say that in rejecting it, and in finding it demeaning to women, feminists are therefore quite simply profoundly *mistaken*. Contemporary culture (the 'inrushing new') must always apparently be seen as more powerful than the living Word of God:

... the content of the symbol 'Father' on the lips of Jesus may be determinatively different from the content of the symbol today... The biblical symbol 'Father' shows no Oedipal content. His children are bound to him by the free choice called 'faith' rather than the enslaving sexual bondage that Freud finds in all modern relationships between parents and children. Therefore, it could be argued that the content of Jesus' 'Father' symbols is so different from the modern symbol 'Father' that Christian liturgy ought to use another symbol for God, one which expresses the joyous liberty of the faith-relationship with a loving sustainer more adequately than Freud's fate-laden 'Father', one that is also less oppressive to females in the light of our changed consciousness in this post-patriarchal era.[52]

Though this kind of writing is presumably what Hamerton-Kelly means when he writes elsewhere of a feminist approach which shows biblical symbolism as 'sexually inclusive and/or beyond sexual differentiation at the deeper level where meaning is effectively located', (an irreproachable objective) it is clear that in practice his way of handling the text is just as selective and as prejudiced as the blue-pencil approach of Grade 2. Just as the Grade 2 approach simply expurgates or otherwise clears away as inoperative (with or without such 'scholarly' justification as may be mustered) all biblical passages which do not pass the test of feminist consciousness, so the Grade 1 approach (at first sight more conservative) seeks to maintain the integrity of the text - in itself a worthy aim - by dissolving away certain levels of meaning in its offending passages, thus, it is hoped, bringing them into line with feminist standards of inspection. So, for Hamerton-Kelly, God the Father becomes a means of resolving human 'Oedipal situations': the Father is a liberating symbol, not a symbol of authority.[53] The Freudian element in Hamerton-Kelly's analysis somewhat obscures his argument: his comment on Isaac's marrying Sarah and finding her love a consolation for the death of his mother ('if ever a statement suggested the need to loosen the bonds of kinship, the need to resolve an Oedipal relationship, it is this one') conveys something of the general flavour.[54] But the overall intention is clear enough. It is to deal with the inescapable fact that, without a massive attempt at Grade 2 censorship, the Father-God symbol simply cannot be avoided in any version of the Christian religion which retains any real working contact with the Bible, and to do so by adjusting the meaning of the symbol so that it may be 'less oppressive to females in the light of our changed consciousness in this post-patriarchal era'. And so, it is not in this view enough to say that the word 'Father' as applied to God by Jesus conveys intimacy ('Abba') and forgiveness, and invites mankind to reconciliation and wholeness; at the same time all emphasis on the necessary *prelude* to that reconciliation, our acceptance of God's authority, must be removed. Thus, Hamerton-Kelly rightly cites the parable of the prodigal son as showing that 'we are free to take our goods and go into a far country', but that 'when we freely return, he welcomes us with joy, and comes to meet us'.[55] What is entirely omitted from his account is the prodigal's consciousness of his own disordered life, his penitence, and his return to filial obedience, becoming 'even as one of thy hired servants'.

What appears to be lacking from such an approach is an inability to perceive that what seem to be emphases contradictory to the modern mind (obedience and liberation) are in fact complementary and mutually necessary. We are freed so that we may become what God intends us to be, not so that we may achieve the fulfilment of our sinful natures as they are: we are liberated in the first place from slavery *to ourselves*. The distinction between 'authoritarian' religion and 'humanitarian' religion proposed by Sölle mirrors precisely the same error, and it results from the same fundamental cause: its liberal protestant hostility to the fundamental and indispensable Christian doctrine that the nature of humankind as we actually see it is deeply flawed, and that without the grace of God it is fatally flawed. And so we can arrive at a theology in which 'obedience' to God is to be *replaced by* 'solidarity' with him, as though these were incompatible goals, as though, indeed, it were possible ever to reach a state of union with God without first overcoming the separation from him caused by our sin and disobedience.

However this may be, it is surely clear that no such one-sided 'humanitarian' theology can be supported by Jesus' use of the term 'Father', or by the cultural context within which its meaning for him (and equally for us) is to be judged. However else we are to describe the father-son relationship as it emerges from the Bible, it is certainly not one the authentic note of which is the encouragement of independent behaviour and autonomous 'personhood' in the son. The behaviour of the prodigal son is *not* a legitimate exercise in self-discovery, but a disordered act of self-will. 'In the biblical literature', write Edwyn Hoskyns and Noel Davey, 'and especially in the New Testament, it is congruity of conduct that marks the relation between father and son and defines the fact of sonship.'[56] Father and son stand within a tradition, which it is the father's part to transmit, and the son's to receive. 'The father commands: the son obeys', as Hoskyns and Davey put it; and they continue:

> Obedience is therefore the characteristic note of sonship. A son reproduces the behaviour of his father because he hears and obeys. The biblical writers therefore depict no straining after emancipation. It is not the duty of a father to train and prepare his son for a time when he will be free to develop his own character, follow his own desires, and work out his own destiny . . . The freedom of a son lies in his recognition of his parentage, not in emancipating himself from it.[57]

It is this expected congruity of conduct between father and son that makes Jesus' astonishing claim 'He who has seen me has seen the Father' (John 14.9) at the same time both shocking and inevitable. It is an assertion of oneness with the divine life; and at the same time a declaration of receptiveness and submission, 'obedience' and 'solidarity' mingling so that they can no longer be distinguished. Whatever else must be said about the relationship of the Father and the Son, this is surely the keynote of Jesus' own understanding of it, and also of that of the New Testament Church. It is the Father who sends the Son (Rom. 8.3); the Father who is the beginning and end of all things (1 Cor. 8.6); and at the end of the ages the Son will submit to the Father, 'the Son will be subjected to him who put all things under him, that God may be everything to everyone' (1 Cor. 15.28).

'That God may be everything to everyone': this submission is not a self-destructive draining of selfhood but the reception of the plenitude of God's generous self-giving. The Son, who is subjected to the Father, and who has subjected us to himself, has thereby given us the glorious liberty of sons of God. By our subjection to him, we are freed from ourselves as we *are*, so that we may become what we should be: 'Truly, truly I say to you, everyone who commits sin is a slave to sin. The slave does not continue in the house for ever; the son continues for ever. So if the Son makes you free, you will be free indeed' (John 8.34-6). And the Son's power to free us in this way flows from his own submission to the Father: 'the Son can do nothing of his own accord, but only what he sees the Father doing; for whatever he does, that the Son does likewise . . . as the Father raises the dead and gives them life, so also the Son gives life to whom he will' (John 5.19,21); 'The words that I say to you I do not speak on my own authority; but the Father who dwells in me does his works' (John 14.10); 'If you keep my commandments, you will abide in my love, just as I have kept my Father's commandments and abide in his love' (John 15.10). Jesus' message is not the *abolition* of subjection and dependence, but their entire redefinition:

> This is my commandment, that you love one another as I have loved you. Greater love has no man than this, that a man lay down his life for his friends. You are my friends if you do what I command you. No longer do I call you servants, for the servant does not know what his master is doing; but I have called you friends, for all that I have heard from my Father I have made known to you. You did not choose me, but I chose you and appointed you that you should go and bear fruit and that your fruit should abide; so that whatever you ask the Father in my name, he may give it to you. This I command you, to love one another. (John 15.12-17)

14
Dealing with Liturgy

If it is true, as radical (Grade 2) Christian feminists claim in common with religious feminists (Grade 3) who have moved beyond what they see as irreversibly patriarchal religions, that the perception of God as *Father* is a projection from a woman-denying patriarchal culture which Jesus saw himself as modifying - even, openly defying - so as to achieve the liberation of women, we would expect to see this shift reflected in his teachings and recorded utterances. As we have seen, we do not; and his most striking failure to assail 'patriarchal' practices and beliefs must surely be judged to be his persistence in the use of the patriarchalist term 'Father' for God. In fact, in the whole of the Old Testament, God is described as 'Father' only eleven times (and not once actually addressed in this way): Jesus, in startling contrast uses the term at least 170 times, and, except for the cry of dereliction from the cross, *always uses this form of address and no other*.[58] It is the way Jesus himself approaches God in prayer, and he invites us, too, to approach him in this way. We are to say '*Abba*, Father', the word a child used to his own father. 'Father' in Christian prayer means, then, love, tenderness and forgiveness together with authority and obedience. The sheer numerical weight of references in the New Testament, both in the sayings of Jesus and in the Pauline epistles, to God's fatherhood, presents radical Christian (or Grade 2) feminists with a problem they have yet convincingly to face. As Hamerton-Kelly rightly says, theology 'is caught between the fact that Jesus expressed his deepest experience of God by means of the symbol "father" on the one hand, and the fact that some women find that symbol demeaning and dehumanizing on the other. This is the issue; it is a real issue. It should be faced in these terms, not confused or evaded'.[59] Whatever we may think of Hamerton-Kelly's own solution of this conundrum, there is no doubt that he has placed the question firmly on the agenda of radical feminist theology. Whether any very convincing response will be forthcoming, however, may be doubted. It is not the radical feminist way: like guerrilla fighters, when faced by a 'combat situation' in which their techniques are powerless, they tend to melt away into the undergrowth to fight again on more promising ground of their own choosing.

From the moment women were ordained to the priesthood in the American Episcopal Church, it became clear that, for some of them at least, the next battle in a long and continuing campaign was to be over the liturgy. At her first Eucharist, concelebrated with her ordaining bishop, one of the most influential of the new women clergy was already moving on to this second stage by arranging the offering of the eucharistic prayer in such a way that the bishop spoke all the parts of the prayer which addressed God as 'Father', leaving her own lips untouched by this oppressive patriarchal symbolism.[60] It is clear why, as the campaign to feminize the Church continued, the liturgy should have become the next battleground; the invading army had moved, as it were on to a bridgehead, a piece of territory it now held: women were, at last, standing at the altar, which they had always seen as a bastion of male power: now they could exercise that power themselves. The liturgy was, literally, in their hands. Certainly, the Bible remained a feminist target: as the Reverend Susan Harris (sometimes addressed as 'Father Susan' put it, 'we can't add to Scripture, but we can manoeuvre it with women's experience to include us'.[61] We have already seen some of the ways in which the theoretical basis for these manoeuvres was established. And though the Bible as a document to be taken as a whole presented obvious difficulties (and few feminists at this stage were advocating actual rewriting of the text), the use of the Bible within the liturgy was an immediately available target; feminist influence in the suppression of, for instance, inconvenient Pauline sentiments was already well established across denominational boundaries. One notable coup, achieved almost unnoticed, has been the optional omission of the verses referring to the headship in Christian marriage of the husband, from the passage in Ephesians (5.2,21-33) which is an appointed epistle in the Roman Catholic nuptial mass.[62]

The Bible, nevertheless, was seen as a difficult and emotional target, and the pitfalls of tampering with it generally understood (reservations which, as we shall see, were to prove well founded). At a time of liturgical experiment and change, however, revolutionary modifications to liturgical texts whose origins are scarcely less ancient or deeply woven into Christian tradition, could more readily be attempted. Such revisions were used without general acceptance, and in circumstances which were not those of normal parish worship. Their aim, however, was clear, and effective resistance to them in official circles apparently non-existent. Their purpose was (and remains) to change the Christian religion, on the assumption that, as Letty M. Russell puts it, since 'theology as practiced in seminaries and pulpits has long been almost exclusively a male domain', it follows that 'conscious and unconscious sexism is reflected in the values, interpretation, and formulation of the Christian faith'. And she goes on to herald a new 'process of interpretation, based on more inclusive use of the ways women and men experience the Christ event'.[63] What, in practice, does this mean? Since seminaries are one of the strategic targets mentioned above, it will not be uninstructive to examine a eucharistic liturgy which has been in use at one of them, the Episcopal Divinity School, Cambridge, Massachusetts. This liturgy is a 'modified' version of the American 1979 *Book of Common Prayer* eucharistic text, and the principles used in the revision are similar to those laid down in several available handbooks and guides; here, for instance are Sharon and Thomas Nuefer Emswiler's criteria for non-sexist hymns, from their book *Women and Worship: a guide to non-sexist hymns, prayers and liturgies* (1974):

1 No masculine words used generically such as 'mankind', 'brotherhood', 'sons of God', and so forth.
2 No masculine references to God such as 'Lord' or 'Father' and no references to God's reign as a 'kingdom'.
3 No masculine references to Christ other than 'he', 'him', or 'his'.
4 No references to the Church or to objects as 'she'.[64]

These criteria are followed closely by the author of this liturgy, the Rev. Carter Heyward (one of eleven women irregularly ordained in 1974) with one exception: no masculine references to Christ whatever (even 'he', 'him' or 'his') have been allowed here. The Nicene Creed emerges from this process of re-orientation in a very curious condition: apart from the suppression of the word 'Father', perhaps the new text's most striking feature is its formal retention of the idea of the incarnation, together with the doctrine's undermining by the suppression of the work 'begotten':

FEMINIST REVISION	ORIGINAL VERSION
We believe in one God, *Holy, Immortal* Almighty, Maker of heaven and earth, Of all that is, seen and unseen. We believe in Jesus Christ, *Image of the invisible God, An eternal showing of the Almighty*, God from God, Light from Light, True God from true God, *caused to become human*, not made, Of one being with the *Almighty*. Through *Christ* all things were made. For us and for our salvation, *Coming to us* from heaven, By the power of the Holy Spirit *Christ* became incarnate *from* the Virgin Mary, and was made *a human being*. For our sake *Christ* was crucified under Pontius Pilate, suffered death and was buried, and on the third day rose again in accordance with the Scriptures; *Christ* entered into heaven *And now has the place of greatest honor with the Holy, Loving, Almighty, Immortal One*. Christ will come again in glory to judge the living and the dead, And of *Christ's reign* there will be no end. We believe in *God* the Holy Spirit, the giver of life, Who *flows forth in the superabundance of love from God Almighty and from the Christ*.	We believe in one God, *the Father*, the almighty, maker of heaven and earth, of all that is, seen and unseen. We believe in *one Lord*, Jesus Christ, *the only son of God*, eternally begotten of the Father, God from God, Light from Light, true God from true God, *begotten*, not made, of one Being with the *Father*. Through *him* all things were made. For us *men* and for our salvation *he came down* from heaven; by the power of the Holy Spirit *he* became incarnate *of* the Virgin Mary, and was made *man*. For our sake *he* was crucified under Pontius Pilate; *he* suffered death and was buried. On the third day he rose again in accordance with the Scriptures; *he* ascended into heaven *and is seated at the right hand of the Father*. *He* will come again in glory to judge the living and the dead, and *his kingdom will have no end*. We believe in the Holy Spirit, the *Lord*, the giver of life, *who proceeds from the Father and the Son*.

With them the Holy Spirit is worshipped and glorified. Through the prophets *God the Holy Spirit* has spoken. We believe in one holy catholic and apostolic Church. We acknowledge one baptism for the forgiveness of sins. We look for the resurrection of the dead, and the life of the world to come. Amen.[65]	*With the Father and the Son he* is worshipped and glorified. *He* has spoken through the Prophets. We believe in one holy catholic and apostolic Church. We acknowledge one baptism for the forgiveness of sins. We look for the resurrection of the dead, and the life of the world to come. Amen.

Nothing could be further away from the atmosphere of profound spiritual reflection surrounding the composition of the Nicene creed than the cold calculation of this revision. 'Criteria' have been applied, stock devices from feminist handbooks deployed: God the Father simply disappears with a stroke of the blue pencil. The resulting document reminds one of nothing so much as a new edition of the Soviet Encyclopaedia, from which all mention of some luminary who has suddenly become a non-person is unaccountably discovered to be eliminated. The objection to this particular expurgation is clear enough: Christian prayer and worship should follow the model of Christ himself, who never used any other form of address than 'Father', and his explicit instructions in his gift of the Lord's prayer. This prompts the question: how does this revision approach the problems posed by this particular prayer? The answer is not uninstructive:

> ABBA, our loving God in heaven, to whom as dear Children we belong, Hallowed be your name, Your realm prevail, Your will be done, On earth as in heaven. Give us today our daily bread. Forgive us our sins, As we forgive those who sin against us. Save us from the time of trial, And deliver us from evil. For yours is the reign eternal in its power and glory now and for ever.[66]

The verbose opening replacement for the simple 'our Father who art in heaven' indicates clearly that though, short of suppressing the prayer altogether there is no way of actually cutting out a word clearly used by Christ himself, and intended by him to be part of a prayer to be used by his followers, this will not be allowed without some accompanying definition. The Aramaic *Abba* is used, frankly, as an evasion; to avoid the hated word 'father' because of its 'patriarchal' overtones, and to replace it with one whose meaning may be more carefully controlled, since it will be less familiar to the congregation. Certainly, 'Abba . . . to whom as dear children we belong' does convey one important layer of meaning (though this is also conveyed by 'Our Father'): 'Abba' is the word used by a child; it is like 'daddy' or the French 'papa'. But these words, as well as conveying tenderness and intimacy should also convey - and would certainly have conveyed to a Jewish child in the time of Christ - the complementary overtones of authority and discipline. 'Abba' is used here, quite simply, because its actual meaning is less widely known than that of 'Father', and it is therefore not generally understood that its indication of gender is just as clear and unambiguous.

The possibilities for sentimentalization and obfuscation opened up by the word 'Abba' are widely recognized by Christian feminists, and its use is recommended, for example in Letty M. Russell's guide *The Liberating Word* (1976), as a means of fulfilling her rule of 'avoiding the use of the words "Our Father", unless they are balanced with other metaphors'.[67] There is little chance of 'balancing metaphors' in the Lord's prayer without some awkwardness. 'Abba' does, strictly speaking, avoid the words 'Our Father'; it is possible to be convinced that 'Abba' has no possible relationship with 'the present meaning of the word "Father"'; honour is satisfied. 'Balancing metaphors', however, is an altogether more satisfying procedure, which is difficult to carry out when simply adapting existing texts. Once these have been abandoned, however, far more imaginative effects may be achieved. Thus, the eucharistic prayer of the Boston version remains, even after its feminist modifications have been applied, relatively traditional in style and even in content. In another eucharistic prayer by the same author (the Rev. Carter Heyward), produced for the 'Well woman center for women and religion' in Philadelphia, such restraints have been removed. The Lord's prayer is now dismantled and partly absorbed into the eucharistic prayer itself, which is composed as a 'litany', with the refrain 'Holy is your name'. It soon becomes clear, indeed, that the entire post-Sanctus of this prayer, which is unusually long, can almost be seen as an attempt to get the Lord's prayer under control, and to answer any notion that Jesus' own name for God might be (as Christians have generally supposed) in some way definitive: by *extending* the prayer in this way, the clear implication is that we must not be satisfied with Jesus' own commands: we must *balance our metaphors*. And so, having first addressed God as *Yahweh*, the prayer goes on to address him as *Abba*:

> Following Jesus, we call you *abba*, for you are like a strong and supportive daddy, protective, encouraging, comforting. Holy is your name.

Now, because metaphors are to be balanced, even the word 'Father' may be employed:

> God our Father, your will be done, on earth as in heaven. We thank you for giving us the bread we need. Holy is your name.

The 'metaphor' is now balanced:

> You hold us in your tender arms like a mother with her newborn infant . . . God our mother, you are the matrix of our power, our tenderness, and our courage. We forget too often that you are God. Holy is your name.

Now, it is clearly implied that in a 'humanitarian' religion, based on solidarity and not on authority, no way of imagining God has priority over any other. God is in everything equally; furthermore, since we are autonomous beings, *our own idea of God is right for us*:

> We know that your names are as numerous and varied as your people, to whom you reveal yourself in different ways so that we may be your co-creative, imaginative, lovers in a world abundant with redemptive images. We see you in the sun and the moon, the rain and the wind, coming with power. We see you in the liberation of humanity from injustice and oppression . . . We see you in our friends and lovers, our spouses and children . . .[68]

It should not be taken for granted, here as elsewhere, that the theological assumptions underlying such writing are so clearly radical or extremist that these assumptions (as well as the highly coloured language in which they are expressed) will necessarily be excluded by those with influence within the Church as a whole, even those whom we might expect to be more theologically conservative. The technique and philosophy of 'balancing metaphors', with all they imply for the Church's theology of God and its attitude to the biblical revelation, may have been *pioneered* by extreme feminists, particularly since the admission of women to priestly orders in the United States, in 1976. But by the early 'eighties, their plausibility was already such that this very radical procedure could be coolly employed by a senior churchman like the Rt Rev. Lyman Ogilby, Bishop of Pennsylvania, in a Eucharistic Preface composed for him. Though Bishop Ogilby was formerly sometimes thought of as a 'moderate', on 6 December 1983 he openly abandoned the ancient and invariable principle governing such composition (restated in a recent mandatory rubric by his province of the Church) that the prayer is to be addressed to the *Father*; and at a Eucharist celebrated before the clergy of his diocese, offered the prayer of consecration to the 'Father of all creation and the Mother of all being'.

15
Perception and Language

What does it *mean* to say that God is our Father? What is the status of such an assertion? Clearly, it cannot be exactly that of a statement like 'John Smith is our father': this would be a limited assertion about the lives of particular people, practically verifiable. Further, both the words 'our' and 'Father' are not merely less personally identifiable, but seem to convey a different kind of meaning; this is signalled in the word 'Father' by its upper-case initial letter. Is it, then, a different *kind* of statement: not one intended to convey in any sense a factual truth, but a comparison: God is *like* our father? This seems a more satisfactory explanation, until we reflect that the power and persistence of this way of thinking of God is unlikely to have been sustained through the centuries by the comparison 'God is like John Smith', infinitely varied and multiplied. We are clearly not intended by Jesus to universalize our own domestic experience, though this is the apparent implication of such feminist objections as Sara Maitland's, to the effect that 'most of us did not experience fathering from our fathers in the terms that Jesus meant when he spoke of God as his "Father" - cradled, fed, played with, and taught'.[69] *This* kind of earthly fathering, was, for Jesus, carried out by his foster-father, Joseph: however successfully this was done, it is clear that Jesus' persistent use of the term 'Father' derives from a vision altogether vaster in its scope than a perception of God as St Joseph writ large.

The idea that *God is our Father* cannot, then, be seen as being simply metaphorical; nor can it be seen as a normally operating factual assertion. In general, however, feminists propose a clear choice between these two alternatives, and then opt without hesitation for the former. This leads to two different approaches. As the introduction to the liturgy of the 'Mother Thunder Mission' explains:

> The first approach points out that masculine imagery and language have been disproportionately used of God and that we need to correct the imbalance by emphasizing the feminine imagery which does not exist in our tradition. Proponents of this view usually argue the importance of God not becoming an 'IT' to us . . .
>
> The other argument stresses that all our talk about God is metaphorical at best. To say that God is a person is not to say 'person as we are'. To use no gender nouns is not to make God an 'it', at least, not in some Christians' experience.[70]

The assumption that 'all our talk about God is metaphorical at best', is one requiring some attention. If this is true, if, that is to say, everything we say about God depends on our power to compare him with something else, it is difficult to know how we are ever to give the word 'God' any meaning or concreteness.

A metaphor (at least as the term is normally understood in this context) is essentially an example of language used horizontally, uniting two or more ideas perceived at the same level of understanding. Certainly, we can understand God in a limited way by the use of metaphor: when we say 'The Lord is my shepherd, I shall not want', we are choosing one aspect of God's relationship with us, and illustrating it by means of a simple analogy. The use of analogical, or simply comparative language about God is useful and inevitable; but it cannot by itself take us far *towards* him, since the ideas thus compared are within the existing boundaries of our understanding. All we can do with this kind of language is to pile metaphor upon metaphor (as in the liturgy quoted above); but still, we will only create a more and more detailed - though possibly inaccurate - map of territory which we already occupy. It will not lead us towards *terra incognita*, towards the God who is not only with us in our trivial daily round, but also *beyond*. We need also a language which functions vertically; one, that is to say, which takes us to the very boundaries of our perception, so that the act of perceiving will always impose inescapably the knowledge that there is more to perceive.

That the mind of industrialized man does not naturally function in this way is clear enough; and it may be that we need look no further for an explanation of the widespread loss of the capacity for belief in God. There has been in our civilization, it is not too much to say, something like a mass failure of imaginative capacity; and perhaps the most striking element in this has been a decay over recent centuries of the instinct, natural in mankind, to perceive things and actions *symbolically*; that is, both as they appear to us and also, and at the same time, as part of an infinitely receding tracery of associated meanings, that extends far beyond our capacity to rationalize or apprehend them.

One easy way to see what has taken place is by observing the way in which popular understanding has changed the meaning of two English words, 'symbol', and 'myth'. A symbol is an image or a concept that contains the power, like a seed, to put down roots to levels of meaning unattainable in a simple prose paraphrase of what the symbol means. A myth is a story which contains within its action key truths about human aspirations and about the human situation itself: it is more true, not less true, than mere fact. What has happened to these two words is profoundly significant. A symbol is now understood either as a kind of shortened code (in the sense in which we say that the elephant is a symbol of the Republican Party), or as a simple metaphor or analogy. A myth is now simply a story which is untrue. The meaning of the two words has been in one case denatured, in the other reversed; and in both, a 'vertical' understanding has been replaced by a 'horizontal' one.

How are we to regain this 'vertical' dimension in our perception? One necessary condition must surely be the willingness once more to bear the uncertainty of standing at the very edge of our understanding, for this is where we shall be led. We need to be able to bear the knowledge (almost unbearable to the modern western mind) of our own extreme finitude. We need, perhaps, to recover in our *thinking* about God, and not only in our attempts to approach him in prayer, what the poet Keats called 'negative capability': 'that is, when a man is capable of being in uncertainties, mysteries, doubts, without any irritable reaching after fact and reason'.[71] And certainly we must wean ourselves from the impulse (surely neurotic in tendency) to reduce our idea of God so that we may *control* it (as we have seen, always a strong feminist instinct). This will not mean a loss of concreteness: on the contrary, as Ernst Cassirer puts it in his *Essay on Man*, 'a religion "within the limits of pure reason" is no more than a mere abstraction. It conveys . . . only the shadow of what a genuine and concrete religious life is.'[72] So, too, we may say, does a *theology* within the limits of pure reason, one which draws such a distinction between the language of prayer and the language of theological reflection that the two become hermetically sealed from each other. One consequence of such an approach may be observed in the fact that the understanding of God as Father, for instance, can be rejected by one distinguished theologian, Professor Maurice Wiles, as a 'primary coordinating concept' on the grounds of its 'lack of conceptual clarity', but accepted in a more spiritual context because it incorporates within the sense

of mystery a 'sense of confidence', and because 'this combination of hiddenness and nearness, of awe and intimacy in the
Christian apprehension of God, needs to find appropriate
embodiment *in the forms of Christian worship*' (my emphasis).[73]
Nothing, surely, could more poignantly illustrate what another
theologian, Fr Andrew Louth, has described as the division in
our times

> ... between theology and spirituality, the division between
> thought about God, and the movement of the heart towards God.
> It is a division between mind and heart, recalling Eliot's
> 'dissociation of sensibility', and a division which is particularly
> damaging in theology, for it threatens in a fundamental way the
> whole fabric of theology in both its spiritual and intellectual
> aspects. Cut off from the movement of the heart towards God,
> theology finds itself in a void - for where is its object? Where is the
> God with whom it concerns itself?[74]

It is clear that the decay in the capacity for symbolic
perception, and the 'dissociation of sensibility' between mind
and heart, are part of the same broad cultural shift. To see
reality symbolically requires precisely the unity of mind and
heart whose absence in theology Fr Louth sees as so damaging: a symbolic perception is one in which all man's diverse
faculties for apprehending reality are brought into play, and
which permits him to transcend the limitations of any merely
rational approach. And so, for instance, the Fatherhood of God
lacks 'conceptual clarity' as a 'primary co-ordinating concept',
since at the merely conceptual level such diverse meanings
within the symbol as the Father's Trinitarian relationship with
the son, the Father's creation of the world, and the Father's
care and nurture of those he has created, simply do not hold
together. But it is surely not at such a level that we should
expect them to hold together, but at one altogether *deeper in*
towards the great *mysterium tremendum et fascinans* of God.
At the level of 'conceptual clarity', a statement such as Christ's
'this is my body', which the priest utters each time he celebrates
the Eucharist, has no meaning at all. It is not a normally
operating factual statement; it can certainly not be seen as a
metaphor or analogy. But, in the words of St Thomas Aquinas,

'faith, the outward sense befriending, makes the inward vision clear':[75] 'this is my body' is a statement simply *beyond the scope* of 'conceptual clarity'; only what the Anglican Collect for Purity calls 'the thoughts of our hearts' can penetrate here. And at this depth there is a known identity between the symbol and the thing symbolized so strong that it can only be dissolved by a clear shift in the way in which reality is perceived, by a withdrawal to the surface where the soil is thin and faith puts down no roots.

When and how the 'dissociation of sensibility' between heart and intellect in Western European culture became effective is problematic. Fr Louth explores its implications particularly from the time of the Enlightenment on;[76] T. S. Eliot himself returns to the English puritanism of the seventeenth century.[77] And certainly, there are rumblings of it much earlier, notably perhaps in the great debate between Luther and Zwingli on the nature of the sacraments, when Luther warned that if Zwingli's reductionist view prevailed, there would be a loss of 'that unity of word and deed, of picture and thing, of the bread and the glorified body: body will become merely body and symbol merely symbol.' As Bishop Michael Marshall comments, 'Luther may have won the debate, but in fact Zwingli has won the day in western culture and thought and not least in theology. Body has become merely body and symbol merely symbol.[78]

16
Returning to the Father

Whether any particular biblical language about God - and most importantly the overwhelmingly preponderant New Testament representation of God as our Father - is to be judged metaphorical or analogical on the one hand, or symbolic in the full sense we have discussed on the other, is therefore clearly a matter of fundamental importance to our wider inquiry. A metaphor, which acts (certainly as the word is normally used in this context) 'horizontally', is within the area of rational apprehension and control. The nature of a symbol is precisely that it takes us beyond this area. A metaphor or analogy may be assessed, and its constituent elements dismantled and adjusted. We may accept or reject it as a matter of rational judgement, as being, or not being, analogically sound. A *symbol* acts at levels of understanding which require acceptance or rejection at deeper levels of the personality than those which can be reached by the intellect alone; and the acceptance or non-acceptance of a *religious* symbol is, to the extent that the symbol is central, an acceptance or rejection of the entire attitude to faith which it embodies. The reason why this must be so is clear: there is in a symbolic understanding, to use Luther's words, a 'unity of word and deed, of picture and thing': and to *reduce* a symbolic understanding to a merely metaphorical one, so that the 'picture and thing' may be brought within the ambit of our critical judgement, and dismantled, assessed, and reassembled at our whim, is no less final than a stark refusal of assent. Once 'body has become merely body, and symbol merely symbol', we are describing - as indeed Luther was in these words - a whole spiritual revolution.

We must establish whether or not language about the Fatherhood of God is to be seen as symbolic in the full sense we have been describing, or simply metaphorical, '*merely* symbolic' (a level at which the term must be used in the context of the knowledge that God is 'beyond human gender'). If we look at the Old Testament references first, the answer seems to be that fatherhood is an analogy, illustrating certain aspects of God's relationship with his people. He is compassionate (Isa. 63.16), and thus like a father; he calls to his people in their faithlessness as a father calls to his child (Hos. 11.1-2); he is Israel's protector, provider and master (Exod. 4.22; Num. 11.12). He is the creator of the nation, to whom the obedience of children is due (Deut. 32.6). At this metaphorical level, no one image can be definitive or complete, and the greater the reality to be described, the larger the plenitude of imagery that will be necessary. For Isaiah, the Father is compassionate, like a merciful judge; but this image from Hebrew culture will not, in such a context, convey *enough*. And so Isaiah adds, like a painter adding colour:

. . . you shall suck, you shall be carried upon her hip,
   and dandled upon her knees,
As one whom his mother comforts, so I will comfort you;
   you shall be comforted in Jerusalem. (Isa. 66.12-13)

This image recalls irresistibly Jesus' words, 'O Jerusalem, Jerusalem . . . How often would I have gathered your children together as a hen gathers her brood under her wings' (Luke 13.34). In one way, it reminds us, too, of the imagery of Julian of Norwich, though it is obvious that her interweaving of analogy and conceptual thinking is of a different order of complexity from anything to be found in the Bible:

> . . . all our life consists of three: In the first we have our being, and in the second we have our increasing, and in the third we have our fulfilment. The first is nature, the second is mercy, the third is grace.
>
> As to the first, I saw and understood that the high might of the Trinity is our Father, and the deep wisdom of the Trinity is our Mother, and the great love of the Trinity is our Lord; and all these we have in nature and in our substantial creation. And furthermore I saw that the second person, who is our Mother, substantially the same beloved person, has now become our mother sensually, because we are double by God's creating, that is to say substantial and sensual. Our substance is the higher part, which we have in our Father, God almighty; and the second part of the Trinity is our Mother in nature of our substantial creation . . .[79]

Whether in Julian's scholastic complexities, or in the simpler imagery of the Old Testament, the important thing to note here is that we are, in all the examples we have so far considered, asked to think of certain clearly defined qualities of God, which are illustrated by saying that he is, in a number of very different ways, *like* a father or a mother. And these analogies are always clearly controlled within definite and evident conceptual limits. God is like a father, or like a mother, because he is strong, or because he feeds his children. But in the Old Testament we are not asked to think of him as actually *being* a father. Man is created in the image of God, and not begotten. By our nature, we cannot actually *be* his children.

When we move from the Old to the New Testament, the

word 'Father' as a name for God takes on an entirely new dimension. The metaphorical level in our understanding of it remains. But added to it now is an element so crucial that we can almost go so far as to say that if we now *only* understand the Fatherhood of God metaphorically, our understanding is less than a fully Christian one: the new element, of course, is Jesus' own use of the term. For at no point does Jesus imply that God is merely *like* a father to him: his message is that in very truth *God actually is his father*. He is begotten, not made. And this understanding is at the heart of the faith of the early Church. As Hoskyns and Davey say, 'the definition of Jesus as the Son of God, and the consequent rider that God is his Father, underlie all the books of the New Testament. These were the fundamental dogmas of primitive Christian theology and ethics.'[80] And the entirely distinctive nature of a father-son relationship (which we have already touched on) was for them part of this perception and at the most profound level, *a level which they clearly saw as including women within its implications for the whole community of faith*. To say, then, that women now need a more androgynous formulation, or that a modern understanding could be equally well conveyed by the quite different relationships 'mother-daughter', or 'father-daughter, or even the indistinct 'parent-child', is tacitly to indicate that the fundamental doctrines of the early Church are no longer available to us, and that we must now create our own. And as part of this perceptual shift, a deep symbolic understanding of God's self-disclosure and redemptive action is reduced to a level at which it may be controlled by human preconceptions: the symbolic has become the merely metaphorical. Here, for instance are two versions of Galatians 4.4-7: First the Revised Standard Version's translation; then the version to be found in the so-called *Inclusive Language Lectionary* also published by the American National Council of Churches, as an epistle for the first Sunday after Christmas Day:

But when the time had fully come, God sent forth his Son, born of woman, born under the law, to	But when the time had fully come, God sent forth the Child, born of woman, born under the law, to

119

redeem those who were under the law, so that we might receive adoption as sons. And because you are sons, God has sent the Spirit of his Son into our hearts, crying, 'Abba! Father!' So through God you are no longer a slave but a son, and if a son then an heir.	redeem those who were under the law, so that we might receive adoption as children. And because you are children, God has sent the Spirit of the Child into our hearts, crying, 'God! my Mother and Father!' So through God you are no longer a slave but a child, and if a child then an heir.

There has occurred, it will be seen, a clear loss of meaning and of spiritual vitality which cannot simply be explained by the fact that the 'inclusive' version shows a clumsiness in handling language not unknown in modern translations. The extent of what has happened is indicated in the first sentence, by the shift from 'his Son' (with all that meant in terms of a father's self-extension and of the congruity of action and of being between father and son) to the bald and virtually meaningless 'the Child'. The loss of the possessive pronoun and the replacement of 'Son' by 'Child' remove any indication of *relationship*; and since the relationship concerned is at the very core of the meaning of this important passage, it is simply reduced to utter *lack* of meaning. Similarly, for God to send 'the Spirit of his Son' into our hearts carries a quite different theological weight and basic sense from sending 'the Spirit of the Child', an expression which is quite devoid of concreteness or incarnational meaning (indeed of any meaning). And there is, in any case, *no question of women being excluded from incorporation into Christ's sonship*: this passage is part of the same sequence of ideas in which Paul has already told us that 'as many of you as were baptized into Christ have put on Christ . . . there is neither male nor female . . . for you are all one in Christ Jesus' (Gal. 3.27-8). As for crying 'God! my Mother and Father!' instead of 'Abba! Father!', nothing could more vividly illustrate the simultaneous distortion and decline in vitality of apprehension, from the symbolic to the metaphorical, from addressing God as actually being (in some way one hardly dares to attempt to understand) one's own Father, to a mere human perception of him as being in some way *like* a parent to us: 'God! My Mother and Father' being simply blasphemous if applied at the level of deep truth demanded by 'Abba! Father!', the level at which Jesus intended us to be drawn - male and female alike - into his own sonship.

The reason for the central position in the faith of the first disciples of God's Fatherhood and Christ's Sonship is very clear. The Father-Son relationship illuminated for them, not the nature of Christ only, but also their own nature, and that of the Church, as well. For Christ's astonishing teaching to them was that because God was *his* Father, he was also *theirs*. This is reflected in the 'impossible' nature of some of Jesus' ethical commands: his intention is that those who follow him shall not merely achieve certain passable standards of ethical conduct, but that, male and female alike, they shall - like sons - show forth the activity of their Father: 'You therefore must be perfect, as your heavenly Father is perfect' (Matt. 5.48). To quote Hoskyns and Davey once more, 'in the biblical literature, and especially in the New Testament, it is congruity of conduct that marks the relation between father and son, *and defines the fact of sonship*' (my italics). The disciples, men and women, are to show the same congruity with the Father's nature as does the Son. And this is why Christ seen as 'Child' only is inadequate to a full Christian understanding, and why 'daughter' would be a plain incoherency: and it is also why feminist resentment at Jesus' inevitable sonship is so grotesquely wide of the mark, for it is precisely the Sonship of Jesus which is the key to our own incorporation, irrespective of sex, into the divine life: there is, we might say, no more striking example of 'sexually inclusive language' in any tongue than the title 'Son of God'. Our very definition of his sonship and ours is to be found in coherence with the divine nature; thus: 'I say to you, love your enemies and pray for those who persecute you, so that you may be sons of your Father who is in heaven; for he makes his sun rise on the evil and on the good, and sends rain on the just and on the unjust' (Matt. 5.44-5). We are to see the activity of God in the world, not only through the mediation of the Son, but through the lives of his disciples, too: 'let your light so shine before men, that they may see *your* good works, and give glory *to your Father* who is in heaven' (Matt. 5.16).

This relationship of children with their Father in heaven is enjoyed by the Christian community, not as members of the human race, but as members of his son's body. It is those who are 'led by the spirit' who are sons of God; 'those who have received the spirit of sonship' will cry 'Abba! Father!',

> . . . the Spirit himself bearing witness with our spirit that we are children of God, and if children, heirs of God and fellow heirs with Christ, provided we suffer with him in order that we may also be glorified with him (Rom. 8.14-17).

With one exception, Jesus is always shown in the gospels speaking of God as Father *only to disciples*: this corresponds with Paul's understanding that 'when the time had fully come, God sent forth his Son . . . *so that* we might receive adoption as sons' (Gal. 4.4-5). There is, between the Father and the disciples, a hidden, though fundamental relationship: 'your Father who sees in secret' (a repeated phrase in Matthew 6) 'knows what you need before you ask him' (Matt. 6.6,8).

At the same time, though there is between Jesus and the disciples a relationship so close that they are commanded to address God as 'Abba', as his adopted sons, Jesus often speaks of himself in relation to the Father in a different way from that in which he describes the Father's relationship with the disciples. Most of the sayings in which we can observe this distinction are those which have to do with his authority and mission, and the *difference* between master and disciples is particularly clear in such passages as Matthew 11.5-7:

> I thank thee Father, Lord of heaven and earth, that thou hast hidden these things from the wise and understanding and revealed them to babes; yea, Father, for such was thy gracious will. All things have been delivered to me by my Father; and no one knows the Son except the Father, and no one knows the Father except the Son and anyone to whom the Son chooses to reveal him.

Despite this obvious and necessary distinction, however, a distinction between the Son, eternally begotten of the Father, and those who have been made sons by adoption and grace, the difference cannot be described as that between fact and metaphor. God is not *like* our Father: through our incorporation into the crucified and risen Christ, we the baptized are now to say that he *is* our Father. What kind of statement can this be? It is not a metaphor; nor, as we have said, is it a normally operating factual assertion. It is, in fact, the same kind of statement as Christ's 'this is my body': a symbolic statement, but not one which is 'merely' symbolic. For the Christian disciple, there is in the vocative 'Our Father' such an identity between the word and the reality that the two cannot be sundered: when a Christian kneels to say the Lord's prayer there is, in Luther's words, 'a unity of word and deed, of picture and thing' that can only be broken by a real loss of contact with a fundamental reality of faith. And it is not a reality the perception of which is *dependent* on such cultural factors as a suitable earthly father-figure for purposes of comparison, any more than the efficacy of the Eucharist depends on the use of bread and wine of suitable quality. It is, on the contrary, by the fatherhood of God that we are to understand and to judge the fatherhood of men: 'call no man your father on earth', says Jesus; 'for you have one Father, who is in heaven'. (Matt. 23.9). The Fatherhood of God is the primary reality; it is the very opposite of a Feuerbachian projection *from* human fatherhood. 'I bow my knees', says Paul, 'before the Father, from whom all fatherhood in heaven and on earth is named' (Eph. 3.14). And there will always be a gap between the earthly realization of the heavenly reality, which makes human fatherhood quite inadequate as anything but a partial analogical model for the Fatherhood of God. Human fatherhood is *judged by* the Fatherhood of God, and this removes from the human father any warrant for unjust domination. On the contrary: the model for the relationship of a father with his children must now be that of the Father with the Son: 'a relationship', as Hoskyns and Davey put it,

> . . . in which what the natural order yearned after but could not satisfy was fulfilled. It is this theme of fulfilment that in the New Testament governs everything that is said - the fulfilment, not only of what has been promised in the Old Testament, but of the yearning of creation itself. The Christians were therefore able to

return to the quite straightforward language of father and son. They had seen an obedience exercised in response to an authority that was not tyrannical; they had seen an obedience wrought out in freedom, not in slavery; and they were persuaded that in the relation of Jesus to God as son to father, the ultimate ground and origin of human life had been revealed.[82]

NOTES TO PART THREE

1 Catharina Halkes, 'The Themes of Protest in Feminist Theology against God the Father', in J.-B. Metz and E. Schillebeeckx, (eds.), *God as Father (Concilium* 143, New York 1981), p. 103.

2 Mary Daly, *Beyond God the Father* (Boston 1973), p. 19.

3 In Carol P. Christ and Judith Plaskow (eds.), *Womanspirit Rising: A Feminist Reader in Religion* (New York 1979), p. 54.

4 The word 'matriarchal', should not, of course, be confused with 'matrilineal' (applied to societies in which descent is traced through the mother) or 'matrifocal' (a matrifocal society is one in which the female role receives special attention or honour). In both matrilineal and matrifocal societies men exercise the governing role.

5 See B. Yorburg, *Sexual Identity* (New York 1975), p. 11.

6 Rosemary Ruether, *New Woman/New Earth* (New York 1975), pp. 13ff.

7 Meinrad Craighead, 'Immanent Mother', in M. Giles (ed.), *The Feminist Mystic* (New York 1982), p. 71.

8 ibid., p. 72.

9 ibid.

10 ibid.

11 ibid.

12 ibid, p. 76.

13 See Carol Christ, *Diving Deep and Surfacing* (Boston 1979), pp. 24, 85.

14 Christ and Plaskow, op. cit., p. 14; Naomi Goldenberg, *The Changing of the Gods* (Boston 1979), p. 103.

15 In *Concilium* 143 (3/1981) p. 64.

16 'Abortion and the Sanctity of Life', in T. Drummond (ed.), *Catholicism and Conflict*, The Jubilee Lectures 1982 (London 1982), p. 51. In 1982, Maitland pointed out, the feast was even more significant, since it 'coincided with the first new moon after the Spring Equinox, a propitious and meaningful day for women'.

17 P. Landes, *Signs* VI (no. 2, Winter 1980), p. 332.

18 John Macquarrie, *Thinking about God* (London 1975), p. 101.

19 *Concilium* 143, op. cit., p. 72.

20 ibid., p. 70.

21 ibid., p. 72.

22 ibid., p. 73.

23 ibid.

24 In *Psychoanalysis and Religion* (New Haven 1950).

25 *Concilium* 143, op. cit., p. 71.

26 Daly, op. cit., p. 97.

27 ibid., p. 33.

28 ibid., pp. 33-4.

29 See M. Stenger, 'A Critical Analysis of the Influence of Paul Tillich on Mary Daly's Feminist Theology', *Encounter* XLIII (Summer 1982), pp. 219-38.

30 P. Tillich, *Systematic Theology* III (London 1963), p. 313.

31 ibid., p. 312.

32 ibid., p. 313.

33 Daly, op. cit., p. 183.

34 ibid., p. 184.

35 In Alan Richardson (ed.), *A Dictionary of Christian Theology* (London 1969), p. 31.

36 ibid.

37 Daly, op. cit., p. 96.

38 Richardson, op. cit.

39 Karl Barth, *The Christian Life (Church Dogmatics IV, 4)* (Edinburgh 1981), p. 51.

40 ibid., pp. 53-4.

41 Daly, op. cit., p. 22.

42 see *Concilium* 143, op. cit., p. 69.

43 Quoted by Karl Barth, in *The German Church Conflict* (London 1965), p. 31.

44 Paul Moore Jr, *Take a Bishop Like Me* (New York 1979), p. 28.

45 Barth, op. cit., p. 32.

46 ibid., p. 30.

47 Goldenberg, op. cit., p. 4.

48 Rosemary Ruether, in *Concilium* 143, op. cit., p. 64.

49 Robert Hamerton-Kelly, in *Concilium* 142, op. cit., p. 95.

50 Moore, op. cit., p. 35.

51 Hamerton-Kelly, op. cit., p. 96.

52 ibid.

53 Robert Hamerton-Kelly, *God the Father* (Philadelphia 1979), esp. pp. 52ff.

54 ibid, p. 33.

55 ibid, p. 81.

56 Edwyn Hoskyns and Noel Davey, *Crucifixion-Resurrection* (London 1981), p. 231.

57 ibid., p. 232.

58 Hamerton-Kelly, *God the Father*, op. cit., p. 20.

59 in *Concilium* 143, op. cit., p. 101.

60 The Rev. Martha Blacklock recalls that 'we divided the Eucharistic prayer so that each of us spoke separately, and I stuck him with all the "Fathers".' Marian Knox Barthelm, 'Priesthood', *New York Times Magazine* (5 September 1982), p. 28.

61 ibid., p. 22.

62 See *People's Daily Missal* (Alcester and Dublin 1974), p. 1712. Verses 23-4 and 33 may be omitted.

63 In Letty M. Russell (ed.), *The Liberating Word* (Philadelphia 1976), p. 88.

64 T. Emswiler and S. Emswiler, *Women and Worship* (New York 1974), p. 108.

65 Unpublished cyclostyled sheet.

66 ibid.

67 Russell, op. cit.

68 As used at the Well Woman: a Center for Women and Religion, 23 May 1982. Unpublished cyclostyled sheet.

69 Sara Maitland, *A Map of the New Country* (London 1983), p. 179.

70 Quoted by Maitland, ibid., p. 172.

71 M. Foreman (ed.), *Letters*, 3rd edn. (London 1947), p. 72.

72 See Ernst Cassirer, *An Essay on Man* (Yale 1944), p. 12.

73 Maurice Wiles, *Faith and the Mystery of God* (London 1982), pp. 118, 95.

74 Andrew Louth, *Discerning the Mystery* (Oxford 1982), p. 2.

75 J. Neale and others (trans.), 'Pange, lingua', *English Hymnal*, p. 326.

76 See Louth op. cit., pp. 17ff.

77 T. S. Eliot, 'Metaphysical Poets', in *Selected Essays* (London 1951), pp. 281-92.

78 Michael Marshall, 'Creation', Loughborough Conference Address, (CLA, London 1978), p. 1.

79 E. Colledge and J. Walsh (ed.), *Julian of Norwich: Showings* (New York 1978), p. 294.

80 Hoskyns and Davey, op. cit., p. 228.
81 National Council of Churches, *Inclusive Language Lectionary, Year A* (Philadelphia 1983), Christmas 1, Lesson 2.
82 Hoskyns and Davey, op. cit., p. 237.

PART FOUR

Femspeak and the New Country

The purpose of Newspeak was not only to provide a medium of expression for the world-view and mental habits proper to the devotees of Ingsoc, but to make all other modes of thought impossible. It was intended that when Newspeak had been adopted once and for all and Oldspeak forgotten, a heretical thought - that is, a thought diverging from the principles of Ingsoc - should be literally unthinkable, at least so far as thought is dependent on words. Its Vocabulary was so constructed as to give exact and often very subtle expression to every meaning that a Party member could properly wish to express, while excluding all other meanings and also the possibility of arriving at them by indirect methods. This was done partly by the invention of new words, but chiefly by eliminating undesirable words and by stripping such words as remained of unorthodox meanings . . .   **George Orwell,** *1984*[1]

Sexist language is an invention of the feminist movement . . . Taken literally [it] is a theory that elevates infantile misunderstandings to the level of hermeneutics. But it would be a mistake to take this literally. It matters little, in the final analysis, that here is a theory of language that rests on little or nothing beyond the emotions of the theorists. What matters a lot is that the theory legitimates a linguistic offensive that is part of a general political strategy. In this strategy, every masculine pronoun purged from a text, every insertion of 'person' as a generic suffix, constitutes a symbolic victory in the larger struggle.
Brigitte Berger and Peter L. Berger, *The War over the Family*[2]

However radicalized feminism may have become since its new awakening among middle-class American women in the early nineteen-sixties, it is to these suburban roots that we must return if we are to approach an understanding of the causes of its immediate impact and continuing influence. Faced by the sheer scale of the historical reinterpretation demanded by later feminisms, and by their proposed radical destruction of so many deeply embedded instincts and habits of mind, the uncomprehending majority of both sexes is liable to dismiss modern feminism as yet another unpleasant and temporary radical aberration, largely invented by a small and unrepresentative coterie, and therefore safely to be ignored. An ideology which trumpets aloud that the family is an instrument of 'patriarchal' oppression, that motherhood is either a form of slavery or a new religion (or both simultaneously) or that all relations between the sexes are - like relations between the classes - a struggle for power, is not likely to be persuasive to more than a very small number of men and women. This does not mean, however, that it can be ignored. A small coterie may (as in such very different though equally crucial matters as liturgical revision and the adjustment of educational programmes) be a vastly influential one, particularly in a society characterized - as most western societies are - by a burgeoning of bureaucratic controls and prescriptions, and of decision-making by small committees, whose composition may be entirely unrepresentative of those whose affairs they seek to regulate.

17

The Problem that Has No Name

It is also clear that, even if we do entirely reject the social, political or theological analyses which emerge from a radicalized liberal feminism, rightly noting their remoteness from the assumptions of most of those whose situation they offer to elucidate, it must also be said that we are not at the same time entitled to assume that the existence of the movement itself is a kind of historical *lusus naturae*; it is evident that, however we assess the accuracy or sanity of its diagnosis, modern feminism is *in its origins* inexplicable except as a response to a real problem, deeply felt by many women.

Its classic expression, of course, is in Betty Friedan's hugely influential book *The Feminine Mystique* (1963), the opening chapter-title of which, 'The problem that has no name', was to contribute an evocative key-phrase to the new movement's growing collection of telling slogans. It was to be rendered obsolete as more radical feminists provided, with very little delay, various names for and analyses of the nameless problem, culminating in the great universal cause of causes, *Patriarchy*: a general diagnosis applicable to all cultures in all ages (except for those feminists resolutely determined to cling to their groundless belief in the existence of earlier matriarchal societies). Unlike later feminisms, Friedan's is attached firmly to a particular society at a particular historical period. 'The problem', she wrote,

> . . . lay unburied, unspoken, for many years in the minds of American women. It was a strange stirring, a sense of dissatisfaction, a yearning that women suffered in the middle of the twentieth century in the United States. Each suburban wife struggled with it alone. As she made the beds, shopped for groceries, matched slipcover material, ate peanut butter sandwiches with her children, chauffeured Cub scouts and brownies, lay beside her husband at night, she was afraid to ask even of herself the silent question: 'Is this all?'[3]

For years, said Friedan, there had been no public acknowledge-
ment of this disquiet. American women were programmed by
countless books and articles to seek fulfilment as wives and
mothers. They were taught how to catch a man and keep him;
how to breastfeed; how to handle such problems as toilet-
training children and coping with 'sibling-rivalry' and ado-
lescent rebellion. They learned, too, such skills as 'how to buy a
dishwasher, bake bread, cook gourmet snails, and build a
swimming pool with their own hands; how to dress, look and
act more feminine and make marriage more exciting; how to
keep their husbands from dying young and their sons from
growing into delinquents'. Apart from the snails and the
swimming-pool, there seems little here which could be represented as trivial, nothing which is not, in fact either desirable or
actually necessary to the good conduct of family life. Most of
these activities (even including the snails) are intrinsically
interesting, and nearly all of them as much or very much more
so than the infinitely less varied functions performed by most
men in their daily work. It has to be said, indeed, that the
achievement of general belief in the greater triviality and
monotony of women's lives as compared with the lives of most
men, is one of the great triumphs of feminist propaganda, and
it is clear that this particular victory is the outcome of a
campaign whose early skirmishes were begun many years
before the shock troops of modern feminism surged over the
barricades to occupy the high ground of enlightened liberal
opinion. In 1910, G. K. Chesterton was already casting a
perturbed gaze over the feminists of his own day; not to
challenge their public campaign for universal suffrage, but to
question the presuppositions which had propelled many of that
generation of aristocratic and upper-middle class feminists into
battle. His most telling criticism, perhaps, was that they had
succumbed to the traditional male view (always denied by
women, and asserted only half-heartedly by men) that the public
arena of the man was a more essential part of the life of the
community than the private domestic world over which
traditionally the woman had always held sway. 'All we men',
noted Chesterton ruefully,

had grown used to our wives and mothers, and grandmothers, and great-aunts all pouring a chorus of contempt upon our hobbies of sport, drink and party politics . . . we told our wives that Parliament had sat late on most essential business; but it never crossed our minds that our wives would believe it . . . Suddenly, without warning, the women have begun to say all the nonsense that we ourselves hardly believed when we said it.[4]

One consequence of this was a growing belief in the relative triviality of the work and concerns of the home, and of all the functions normally performed by women. It is here that Chesterton is at his most incredulous. What does it mean, he asks, to say that the work of the household is drudgery?

If drudgery only means dreadfully hard work, I admit the woman drudges in the home, as a man might drudge at the Cathedral of Amiens or drudge behind a gun at Trafalgar. But if it means that the hard work is more heavy because it is trifling, colourless and of small import to the soul, then . . . I give it up; I do not know what the words mean. To be Queen Elizabeth within a definite area, deciding sales, banquets, labours and holidays; to be Whiteley within a certain area, providing toys, boots, sheets, cakes and books, to be Aristotle within a certain area, teaching morals, manners, theology and hygiene; I can understand how this might exhaust the mind, but I cannot imagine how it could narrow it. How can it be a large career to tell other people's children about the Rule of Three, and a small career to tell one's own children about the universe? How can it be broad to be the same thing to everybody, and narrow to be everything to someone? No; a woman's function is laborious, but because it is gigantic, not because it is minute.[5]

While men are expected to be (and by temperament, we might add, are generally more suited to be) specialists, uniquely - perhaps obsessively - confined to one particular function, women must be infinitely more variable. 'Tradition has decided', as Chesterton puts it, 'that only half of humanity shall be monomaniac . . . it has decided that this specialism and this universalism shall be divided between the sexes. Cleverness shall be left for men and wisdom for women'.[6]

This is all, surely, well said, though we may note that Chesterton's argument depends to some extent on certain underlying conditions which can less and less be relied on to obtain, and on certain presuppositions which seventy-five years later are considerably weaker in most advanced western countries. The change can be summed up briefly by saying that women are in general more isolated by domestic life than they were, and that the nature of their work has (in many different ways) been to some extent mechanized and thus denatured. This is true of all social classes. The middle-class household, presided over by the mistress of the house and comprising as well as children (with nanny or nursemaid), servants and surviving grandparents, has now disappeared: its modern equivalent is a wife alone with her children (when they are not at school or playgroup), her servants replaced by machines, her parents living either far away or in an old people's 'home'. The working-class wife of Chesterton's day lived a more arduous life, but one in which she was sustained by being a member of a real community of a kind which has now all but disappeared. It was the community most vividly portrayed for modern audiences, perhaps, by the television programme *Coronation Street*, a series whose enduring appeal has been its unsentimental realism combined with a component of nostalgia which has grown more powerful as the old streets have been torn down and replaced by high-rise council flats. Here, too, the life of the woman has become more isolated, more mechanized, and more desolate. Her children play, out of sight far below; she does not speak to her neighbours; no one calls at the door; the building falls into ever greater disrepair.

The life of western women has undoubtedly, in the second half of the twentieth century, developed in many directions which have led to the traditional functions of women in the family and in society becoming in some ways denatured, isolated and undervalued; and there can surely be little doubt that it is to these developments that we must to no small extent attribute the increasing plausibility during this period of the modern feminist movement, and the often passionate conviction of the support it has attracted, particularly among articulate middle-class women.

And perhaps the most important fact to assert here (or at any rate the most germane to the present discussion) is that the negative effects of these developments on women were entirely unintended and largely unforeseen. There has been no conspiracy; the male sex has not (consciously or unconsciously) used its skills to create new conditions of serfdom for women. On the contrary: the mechanization of domestic tasks was intended to free them from drudgery. The invention of the cake-mix and the TV dinner (to take one trivial example) may have removed the satisfaction of cooking; but their intention was to lighten women's burdens.

And here is a great irony: for the assumption of an expressly (though not always consciously) engineered male dominance is precisely the fundamental presupposition of the new feminism that has flourished under these new conditions. And as the movement grows more radical, so the feminist indictment of the male sex extends its political, historical and (most radical of all) its theological scope far beyond the immediate conditions in modern industrial society which gave it its initial persuasiveness. The condition of women today is seen less and less as a function of life in an impersonal and despiritualized industrial society, more and more as the direct result of a 'patriarchal' oppression, exercised at the level of conscious policy, and stretching back to the dawn of history. Women, it is asserted, are trapped inside artificially constructed stereotypes, designed to maintain their dedication to the satisfaction of male needs and the perpetuation of a generally higher level of life for the male sex. There is also a male 'stereotype': but it is that of the overlord, and not, like the wife's, of the serf. The difficulties of being a *man* in modern industrial civilization (or in any other) are rarely either discussed or even recognized, except in some such canting formula as 'men also need to be liberated from the intolerable burden of being oppressors'.

And here, surely, we have penetrated to the shifting sands which underlie the foundations of the forbidding and seemingly unassailable palace of feminist culture. If we live in a society in which men oppress women to their own advantage, where are their advantages? Of what do they consist? If the satisfaction and dignity of women's lives has been drained away, is this because there is, as it were, a static quantity of these commodities, which men have siphoned off into their already overflowing reservoirs? It requires, surely, a consciousness which has been in some way removed from reality (whether 'raised' or not is another question) to be able to give the standard feminist reply. For if one thing is surely obvious about modern societies, it is that no one sex has a monopoly in lives without spiritual meaning, or in the first-hand knowledge that a mass civilization has somehow come to control human existence in many unacceptable ways. If we need a sexually-based 'conspiracy to oppress' theory, that of Esther Vilar in *The Manipulated Man* (1971) is just as plausible as any of the feminist models:

> No matter what a man's job may be - book-keeper, doctor, bus driver or managing director - every moment of his life will be spent as a cog in a huge and pitiless system - a system designed to exploit him to the utmost and to his dying day . . . a man is like a child who is condemned to play the same game for the rest of his life. The reason is obvious: as soon as he is discovered to have a gift for one thing rather than another, he is made to specialize. Then, because he can earn more money by working in that field, he is forced to do it forever . . . Therefore he will add up figures, press buttons and add up more figures, but he will never be allowed to say: 'Enough of this. I've had it! Now I'll do something else'. The woman who is exploiting him will not *really* permit him to look for something else . . .[7]

Whatever we may think of Vilar's view of the specific responsibility of women for the way in which men have to live their lives, we must surely recognize this as an authentic enough general picture of the way in which very many, and possibly most men have to live in the world's advanced countries. Unless, that is, we see the world through the intervening lens of 'feminist consciousness'; in that case we will continue to insist on our own version of reality. As Arianna Stassinopoulos puts it, radicalized feminists 'are only able to do this because they are so obsessed with the "wrongs" of women that they never really come to terms with the question of what life is like for men.'[8] Men are just as emotionally vulnerable;

indeed, Stassinopoulos goes on, in most ways they are more vulnerable than women. There are more male miscarriages and stillbirths. Infant mortality is higher among males, and male mortality is higher throughout childhood. More boys than girls are referred to the child psychiatric services, and the more severe the disorder, the higher the proportion of males. Above all, women today live longer, often very much longer, a fact which Stassinopoulos sees as especially telling: 'If it is the result', she says, 'of innate differences between the sexes, the Women's Lib thesis that all sex differences are culturally determined collapses; if it is the result of environmental factors, then men are more harshly treated than women and it is their myth of the downtrodden woman that collapses.'[9]

18

Feminist Consciousness and the Reconstruction of Reality

There are, certainly, some signs that a handful of the first generation of modern feminists has begun to perceive that things are not quite as they supposed. As more and more women have successfully launched themselves into careers once the almost exclusive preserve of the males, so, increasingly, difficult questions and hard realizations have begun painfully to surface; at any rate for the generation of feminists who span the old world, in which the family was the largely unquestioned hub of female creative activity, and the new world in which (at any rate in publicly declared conventional wisdom) it is a compromised and failing institution, simply one model among others as a framework for human association and child care. Perhaps it is Betty Friedan, who more than any other woman helped to shatter the old consensus, who most poignantly expresses these doubts. 'Are men and women moving in opposite directions', she now asks,

. . . chasing illusions of liberation by simply reversing roles that the other sex has already found imprisoning? Maybe there are some choices we, they, don't want to face, or shouldn't have to face. Maybe they are not real choices - not yet, not the way society is structured now, or not ever, in terms of basic human reality . . . *I hear now what I would not let myself hear before* - the fears and feelings of some of those who have fought our movement. It is not just a conspiracy of reactionary forces . . . (my italics)[10]

There are no signs, however, that such questioning is anything but very rare among the great majority of those committed to the feminist vision. Most obviously, because there has been since the publication of *The Feminine Mystique* a marked radicalization of Friedan-style liberal feminism: commitment is more rigidly ideological, anything that smacks of compromise less tolerated. And underlying the feminist world-view, indeed in a real sense creating it, is the kind of psychological underpinning normally associated with religious faith. The attainment of *feminist consciousness* is not merely a matter of accepting a particular analysis of women's place in this or any other civilization. It is a new vision, which excludes all others. 'I hear now', says Betty Friedan, 'what I would not let myself hear before'. But feminist consciousness is more than a mere stopping of the ears, though it has to be said that it is that at the very least. But there is more: once the individual feminist has been through the process known as 'consciousness-raising', particularly by attending the women's groups whose purpose is to produce and maintain this psychological effect, it is not merely her understanding of social relationships which has changed, but her whole perception of reality. She has undergone a kind of *metanoia*, or conversion. Suddenly, all the frustration and spiritual emptiness she felt before has been given a reason: patriarchy. It no longer occurs to her (if ever it did) that Friedan's agonized question about her life as a woman in twentieth-century America, 'is this all there is?' is one asked with equal pain by men too, and that it is a questioning inseparable from the human condition itself: throughout human history, men and women have experienced the restlessness and longing that comes from the knowledge that human life as we experience it is somehow not what human life was intended to be. The Christian answer to the conundrum has always been clear: our *lives* are not what they should be because *we* are not what we should be. And for Christians this is not in the end a pessimistic answer, since through Christ's incarnation, death and resurrection we have been given the means to overcome our human limitations and to attain at last what all human beings long for, whether they know it or not: the vision of the glory of God in the face of Jesus Christ. 'O God, thou hast made us for thyself', prayed Augustine; 'our souls are restless until they rest in thee'.

From a Christian perspective, then, the cardinal error of feminism is to ask an essentially religious question, 'is this all there is? What is wrong with my life?' and to give it a merely secular answer. The fact that the secular explanation is itself based on a misapprehension compounds the error. And the effect of this double error when applied by women to their religious faith is predictable. For the secular answer that emerges from the feminist consciousness is that the fundamental problem is not to be found within, but is to be laid at the door of certain external socio-political structures, imposed by an identifiable external human enemy. And at the point at which this answer is accepted, the journey of the soul towards God is halted, perhaps even reversed, since an essential impulse towards movement is now lacking: all the natural human instincts to resist personal change have received a fatal boost. This is how one woman described the experience of leaving the Roman Catholic Church and becoming a feminist to a 'public hearing' organized by Catholic feminists in 1980:

> Last fall, I experienced a ten-week consciousness raising seminar for women sponsored by the National Organisation for Women. It was a painful but beautiful experience, discovering a new reality and support for my true inner feelings. For the first time in my life, it was OK to be feeling whatever I was feeling. I began to see the impossible situation of women existing in a society ruled by men and male gods. And the real issue is the overwhelming denial of power to women.[11]

To the question posed by the conference, 'Woman and Roman Catholic: Is it Possible?' she answered with 'a very emphatic "No"'. 'Women's spirit has been stifled too long', she continued:

> I feel it's time to begin to celebrate ourselves, our own spirituality; to learn to do things for our own reasons and to measure ourselves by our own standards; to create loving support groups which allow for a free self-development; to realize our own inner creative force, which, I think, is our true image of God.[12]

The incompatibility between the Christian tradition as it has been understood from the beginning, on the one hand, and a radicalized feminism, on the other, is clear to most radical feminist Christians, who have generally come to the conclusion that they have two alternatives: to leave the Church, or to find ways of transforming Christian tradition. There are two ways in which this last alternative is argued to be legitimate: either by claiming that the tradition as we have it is not the true tradition (evidence of female leadership and female oriented teaching having been weakened or suppressed); or while accepting that the tradition is more or less accurately transmitted maintains that it is *ab initio* deeply suspect, but nevertheless contains within itself the seeds of its own revolutionary transformation. In either case, the more of the existing tradition that can be claimed as corrupt or inaccurately transmitted by 'androcentric' minds, the greater the scope for 'reconstruction', a conveniently ambiguous word conveying not only demolition and rebuilding but also, as in archaeology, the rediscovery of origins by imaginative extrapolation from such evidence as has survived time and other ravages: in this case the ravages concerned include the dissolving acids of feminist censorship.

The implementation of 'reconstruction' in this second meaning may be observed taking place in an interesting way in Elisabeth Schüssler Fiorenza's book *In Memory of Her: a feminist theological reconstruction of Christian origins* (1983), hailed by the *New York Times* as 'feminist theology come of age'.[13] Fiorenza's contention is that the 'androcentric' character of the biblical texts makes them unacceptable as they stand. Because they were written by men, all the writings collected in the New Testament have weakened the evidence of women's central place in the early Church in various ways. The story of female leadership in the early Christian movement is a largely untold one which must be 'creatively' disinterred:

> Androcentric texts are parts of an overall puzzle and design that must be fitted together in creative critical interpretation. It is crucial, therefore that we challenge the blueprints of androcentric design, assuming instead a feminist pattern for the historical mosaic, one that allows us to place women as well as men into the center of early Christian history. Such a feminist critical method could be likened to the work of a detective insofar as it does not rely solely on historical 'facts' nor invents its evidence, but is engaged in an imaginative reconstruction of historical reality.[14]

This method, says Fiorenza, is 'an act of feminist transformation'. What does this all mean? She provides us with an example of the way in which 'androcentric design' has operated on the gospels' historical raw materials at the very beginning of her book. In all four gospels, there are versions of a story of a woman who anoints Jesus. According to Luke, this anointing was of Jesus' feet. Why, asks Fiorenza, should this be recorded? The anointing of a guest's feet was a commonplace gesture. But Jesus, in Mark's version, is recorded as saying that 'wherever the gospel is preached in the whole world, what she has done will be told in memory of her'. Is it not much more likely that the woman's action was an anointing of Christ's *head*, a prophetic gesture proclaiming recognition of his kingship? But, says Fiorenza, 'it is obvious that the redactional retelling of the story seeks to make the story more palatable to a patriarchal Greco-Roman audience.' Luke discredits the woman by making her a sinner; all three synoptic gospels suppress the woman's name: 'the name of the betrayer is remembered, but the name of the faithful disciple is forgotten because she was a woman'. Most telling of all, the prophetic character of her action is hidden; a kingly anointing is changed in the telling to a mere oiling of feet. But all is not lost: 'Christian feminist theology and biblical interpretation are', says Fiorenza, in the process of rediscovering that the Christian gospel cannot be proclaimed if the women disciples and what they have done are not remembered. They are in the process of reclaiming the supper at Bethany as women's Christian heritage in order to correct symbols and ritualizations of an all-male Last Supper that is a betrayal of true Christian discipleship and ministry.[15]

It is certainly true that one of Fiorenza's criteria for feminist biblical criticism, that it should not invent its evidence, has been observed in her reconstruction of the story of the anointing of the Lord's feet, since she produces no evidence of any kind whatever. But then, this method 'does not rely solely on historical "facts"' (note the scant regard for facts implied by those quotation marks); the aim is to 'place women as well as men into the center of early Christian history'. And this (understood in a modern feminist sense) is the *primary* aim. If it can be achieved in a scholarly manner, all well and good. But in the end, the truth is what 'feminist consciousness' says it ought to be. And so, says Fiorenza elsewhere, though suggestions of female authorship for parts of the New Testament, such as Adolf Harnack's contention that Priscilla and Aquila are the most likely authors of Hebrews (which she believes has 'great historical probability') are not in themselves helpful, since women as well as men were 'socialized into the same androcentric mind-set', *nevertheless*, 'it seems helpful to conjecture female authorship for early Christian writings *in order to challenge the androcentric dogmatism that ascribes apostolic authorship only to men.*'[16] The issue has become, now, not whether or not such suggestions are *true*, but which of the various possibilities is most useful to the feminist case. And, on the whole, Fiorenza concludes that 'the suggestion of female authorship . . . has great imaginative-theological value because it opens up the possibility of attributing the authority of apostolic writings to women and of claiming theological authority for women'.[17] What we need to know is not what actually was the case, but what should have been the case. The purpose of scholarship has become, not the discovery of truth, but the nurture of feminist consciousness. And so, to 'relativize the impact of androcentric texts and their unarticulated patriarchal mind-sets'[18] on her students, Fiorenza, who holds the position of Professor of New Testament Studies and Theology at the University of Notre Dame, has found it helpful to encourage them to write 'apocryphal' texts from the perspective of leading women in early Christianity. One of these, a letter from the 'apostle' Phoebe, she reproduces in full. It is some 1200 words long, and it opens as follows:

> Phoebe, an apostle of Christ Jesus by the will of God, called to preach the Good News, to all the saints, my sisters and my brothers, who are at Cenchreae:
>
> Grace to you and peace from God our Creator, Jesus our Wisdom, and the Spirit our Power . . . May God, Mother and Father, Friend and Consoler, fill you with all love, all gentleness, all joy . . .[19]

Like others we have considered, this is a good example of what Brigitte and Peter Berger have tellingly named 'femspeak', though here we are dealing with a phenomenon whose implications are much more potentially radical, *theological* Femspeak. Like the examples we have already considered it obeys all the criteria of Orwell's 'Newspeak'. Its purpose is gradually to render non-feminist thought, in Orwell's words, 'literally unthinkable, at least so far as thought is dependent on words'. Like Newspeak it operates 'chiefly by eliminating undesirable words and by stripping such words as [remain] of unorthodox meaning'.[20] Here, the expression 'God the Father' has been rendered safe by eliminating 'Father' and replacing it with a permitted alternative; 'Son' for Jesus has been similarly processed. The 'Father' which does appear has been 'stripped of unorthodox meanings' by the process of 'balancing metaphors'; all these, of course, are techniques we saw in the last section being applied to actual liturgical and biblical texts. In this 'apocryphal' text, we move one stage further: just as language has been purged, so too has the frustrating effect on the mind of bourgeois ideas about evidence or probability. 'Phoebe's letter' continues with an account of the doings of some of the other Apostles. Paul has been tiresome, though 'despite our difficulties, we did embrace and commend each other to God': Paul, though limited, and given to 'returns to the past before he received the freedom of the spirit', nevertheless believes that if any of his letters happens to survive, 'only someone bewitched will fail to see the difference between my preaching of the Good News and my ramblings about cultural problems and situations'.[21] It is Peter who is the real threat, continually squabbling with the 'apostle' Mary Magdalen:

> Peter so stubbornly refuses to listen to Mary, even though he himself so often tells how she brought him the first news of the Risen Lord. Mary's patience has been exemplary - Peter can be infuriating at times yet she always responds calmly. It can only come from her confidence born on that Easter Sunday morning. What a source of encouragement she is to all the saints, and what a privilege her community has in having such a leader.[22]

The primary aim of this exercise, Professor Fiorenza clearly implies, is a psychological one. Its aim is to make imaginatively vivid to a 'raised consciousness' the kind of assumptions which require to be made if Christian origins are to be reconstructed in the feminist mould. It is a conscious exercise in myth-creation, put together, in her own words, 'in order to break the hold of the androcentric text over our historical imagination'.[23] It is, quite simply, the controlled manipulation of historical assumptions in the service of ideology: a technique not unknown to the twentieth century, and employed with sinister effect by more than one oppressive government. And this proceeding is not to be excused by saying, as Professor Fiorenza does elsewhere, that 'scholars have widely abandoned' the notion of history as 'what actually has happened.'[24] Certainly, this is very far from being *all* that history is. The way in which events are related will inevitably reflect the interests and presuppositions of the historian. But once these become *dominant*, what we have ceases to be history at all in any generally accepted sense. To say that history is more than 'what actually has happened' is not to say that it is quite *independent* of what has happened, or that the values and interpretations of the historian may ever be so evidently unassailable as to warrant a conclusion being reached as to historicity *primarily* on ideological grounds. This appears, however, to be Fiorenza's basic assumption. Hence, she baldly informs us - having decided that the New Testament documents are suspect because they are not based on her own pre-suppositions (Fiorenza calls this the 'feminist hermeneutics of suspicion') - that

> Androcentric texts and documents do not mirror historical reality, report historical facts, or tell us how it actually was . . . Such texts must be evaluated *historically* in terms of their own time and culture [i.e. dismissed as androcentric] and assessed *theologically* in terms of a feminist scale of values.[25]

This is not to abandon the idea of revealed truth, it will be seen: it is to appropriate it for other uses. Certainly, the idea (which until this century has united all Christians however divided they were on other issues) that the biblical texts, and especially the New Testament, embody in a variety of different ways a substantially viable record of God's self-revelation to humanity, has entirely disappeared: but it has been replaced by a new theory of revelation. The truth is now vouchsafed to those granted feminist consciousness, who may now, by the use of 'historical imagination' reunite us with our true origins and who, by applying a 'feminist scale of values' will be the appointed arbiters of the new orthodoxy.

19
The Big Lie

The 'feminist hermeneutics of suspicion' can be relied on to operate, it will be seen, without using any of the overt techniques for establishing a non-androcentric 'mind-set' outlined by Fiorenza. Once induced, feminist consciousness proceeds unaided to select, suppress, imagine and misunderstand its way to a unified vision of religious or social realities. The problem of clearing the ground for feminist 'reconstruction' simply takes care of itself. The entire Christian tradition (from which - as a matter of actual historical fact - women have emerged with a more honoured position than that created for them in any other world religion, with the possible exception of Judaism, another 'patriarchal' faith) emerges from scrutiny 'in terms of a feminist scale of values' as a sustained and consistent tool of patriarchy which, having seized control of the movement at the very outset with remarkably little difficulty soon after its inception, maintained its misogynist character with little resistance through the ages until the present day. As Rosemary Ruether explains it, 'Males, as the monopolizers of theological self-definition, project onto women their own rejection of their "lower selves". Women, although equivalent in the image of God, nevertheless symbolize the lower self, representing this in their physical sexual nature.'[26] Woman in this view, which Ruether claims as 'classical orthodoxy' has a lesser spirituality and a greater aptness for sin. She is, quite simply, a lesser being. And 'this pattern of patriarchal anthropology can be illustrated in the entire line of classical Christian theology from ancient to modern times.'[27] Ruether goes on to single out for special attention four key figures, Augustine, Aquinas, Luther, and Barth[28] (all well-established names in feminist demonology).[29]

If this were indeed the clear, consistent and unambiguous teaching of the Christian tradition about women, it is remarkable how little adverse effect it appears to have had on the attitude towards women of Christian men through the ages, as we can see it reflected in literature, art and actual behaviour, and as we may compare it with that of other traditions. Ruether, of course, does not quite say that this contemptuous view is the *only* Christian teaching about women; but it can be '*illustrated* in the entire line of classical Christian theology'. Examples, that is to say, may be found. Her implication, of course, is that these examples represent the dominant and continuing tradition, one so strong that it remains a major problem for women in the Church today; and the importance in Christian tradition of the four teachers she singles out here to exemplify this tradition is clearly intended to underline this implication.

How true is it, in fact, that these writers *are* all misogynist? How clear is it, first, that apparently misogynist passages quoted from their works are central to their teaching on the relations between the sexes taken as a whole; and how clear is it, secondly, that these passages are in all cases actually misogynist at all? As we have seen, there is nothing quite like a 'feminist consciousness' for assuming a 'chauvinist put-down' where none is intended. The standard feminist case against St Thomas Aquinas, for instance, centres on his adoption of Aristotle's definition of woman as a 'misbegotten male'.[30] Undoubtedly, this sounds offensive on a first reading; it *continues* to be offensive only if we are so sure we know what this means that we do not bother to find out. In fact, it is a simple reflection of a primitive biology according to which female offspring are produced by an intervention in the normal process of reproduction, which, it was held, otherwise produced male offspring. It is in fact, as one writer has suggested, 'fairly close to the modern understanding of the generation of males. Male characteristics are produced in a foetus when the normal sequence of producing a female foetus is interrupted by the secretion of male hormones. To use an Aristotelian terminology, according to modern science, the male is a misbegotten female.'[31]

Suppose, however, that we were to continue to assume that Aquinas's expression 'misbegotten male' *should* be taken at face value. Would this show that the overall tendency of Thomist theology, with all its vast influence on Christian tradition, has been to devalue women? As Mary Daly herself pointed out while still a comparatively 'moderate' feminist attempting to salvage the Church for feminism, Thomas taught that the rational soul is not transmitted by the reproductive process but rather is directly infused by God. Further, he held that intellectual understanding and the will are entities independent of the bodily organs. 'It is abundantly clear', she goes on,

> ... that ... according to Thomas's own principles, the alleged defectiveness of women, both as to their own role in generation and considered as products of the generative process, becomes extremely difficult to uphold. Indeed, in the light of these principles it becomes impossible to uphold. According to Thomas, it is the intellectual soul which makes the human person to be the image of God. This is neither caused by the male, nor is it essentially different in man and woman.[32]

This, of course, comes from *The Church and the Second Sex* (1968). By 1973, her relatively traditional equal rights feminism having been considerably radicalized, she is able to move beyond such confusing reservations. Her attitude, not only to Thomas but to the whole Judaeo-Christian tradition, has now become thoroughly informed by 'the feminist hermeneutics of suspicion', to the point at which she has left the Church whose entire tradition is, for her entirely beyond doubt, overwhelmingly hostile to women:

> The history of anti-feminism in the Judaeo-Christian heritage already has been exposed. The infamous passages of the Old and New Testaments are well known. I need not allude to the misogynism of the Church Fathers for example, Tertullian, who informed women in general: 'You are the devil's gateway', or Augustine, who opined that women are not made to the image of God. I can omit reference to Thomas Aquinas . . . who defined women as misbegotten males . . .[33]

And so on. The Christian tradition is so thoroughly and so clearly established as anti-woman that there is now, for her, scarcely any need to mention the details, and certainly none to look more deeply into the complexities of context and background informing them. Her earlier and equally clear belief that, so far as Thomas Aquinas is concerned, at least, the 'deep roots of Thomas's thought . . . clearly support the genuine equality of men and women . . .',[34] is now quite eradicated.

Daly's earlier judgement on the overall tendency of St Thomas's thought is, nevertheless, surely correct, and it seems to me equally relevant to all the other examples of alleged misogyny just quoted. Certainly, anyone wanting to assemble 'evidence' of Christian misogyny may easily make out a circumstantial case (though rather less consistently than if he were looking for examples from feminist writers showing a loathing and suspicion of all men). But what we need to understand is not whether, in a tradition five thousand years old, male (and female) irritation with the opposite sex has or has not surfaced from time to time (as in any normal successful marriage); what we need to penetrate are, to use Daly's phrase, the '*deep roots*' of Christian teaching on the relations of men and women. If Tertullian is quoted on woman as the 'devil's gateway', as he is by Ruether, Daly and others, let him also be shown (as he never is by feminists) addressing them in the same work, *De Cultu Feminarum*, as 'Handmaids of the living God, my fellow-slaves and sisters';[35] and let his teaching on the husband's authority over the wife be understood clearly in the context of the deeply moving picture of mutual conjugal affection and respect he paints elsewhere:

> How can we be equal to the task of singing the happiness of a marriage which the church unites, the Eucharist confirms, the blessing consecrates, the angels proclaim, the Father ratifies? . . . What is the tie of two believers with one hope, one discipline, one service? They are siblings; they are fellow slaves; there is no separation of spirit or flesh . . . Together in the church of God, at the banquet of God, in anxieties, in persecutions, in joys; no one hides any thing, avoids the other, or is disagreeable to the other . . .[36]

The one-sided feminist treatment of Tertullian is exactly paralleled by that meted out to Augustine (an important strategic target) who is represented by Daly as maintaining baldly that women are not in the image of God; Ruether quotes (as exhibit A in this indictment) the passage from *De Trinitate* in which Augustine says that the husband together with the wife is the image of God, but that the wife, 'when she is referred to separately *in her quality as helpmeet, then* she is not the image of God' (my italics).[37] *Is* this a statement that the woman *as a woman* is not in the image of God and that she is therefore man's inferior? Ruether assumes without further discussion that it is, though Augustine is involved here in an argument *whose purpose is precisely to maintain that in 1 Corinthians 11.7 Paul does not intend to say that women are inferior to men, but different:* Woman is a human being in parity of nature with man.[38] As in her references to Aquinas and to Tertullian, Ruether excludes any information on the particular context of this passage within the work itself, or any kind of attempt at a balanced assessment of the general tendency of the life and work of the writer as they affect the status of women. And in the case of Augustine, too, the truth is less simple than the feminist caricature. To balance Ruether's view, it may be useful here to cite that of Niceto Blazquez, who at the end of a substantial study of the question of Augustine's attitude to women concludes that

> . . . there exists no foundation whatever in Augustinian thought for discriminating against the woman with respect to the man. Both are equally and naturally 'in the image of God' by virtue of their rational soul. Although the Augustinian mental scheme is from time to time somewhat Platonic, the content of Augustine's teachings is always Christian and founded on Holy Scripture. This is so much the case that he even came to say of Plato himself that he offended the human race with his mode of thought on women.
>
> When Augustine speaks of the subordination and obedience of the woman, always within the matrimonial context, this is understood in the Christian sense, and presupposes the context of the love preached by Christ, in which to serve is to reign and slavery is transformed into liberty.
>
> Even omitting the existence of the love which gives sense to many things that without it have none, we always stumble across the nature, in herself, of the woman as image of God, which makes absolutely impossible any imaginable form of adverse discrimination with respect to men.[39]

And these last two paragraphs may surely be taken also as being generally true of the Christian tradition itself, once we have accepted the great and indispensable Pauline teaching - discussed in an earlier chapter - that within the Christian dispensation authority and equality may subsist together, not as warring and contradictory principles, but as necessary and complementary foundations of an authentically Christian ecclesial and social order. Man and woman, husband and wife are now 'subject one to another', and this is the meaning of the man's vocation to headship. In Tertullian's words, they are 'fellow slaves'. To perceive this, however, requires a major shift away from any existing secular understanding (and above all any contemporary political understanding of either left or right), of such words as 'authority' and 'equality'. And this cannot be achieved without an authentic theological understanding of the Christian community's apartness from all the world's values as the necessary basis for its authority to speak prophetically about the world's affairs: the prophet comes in from the desert, where he has been speaking with God; and he challenges a rebellious and sinful generation to return to obedience to him.

It has to be said that on this acid test the feminist movement within the Church is the very opposite of prophetic. Though far from 'secular' in the sense of denying the religious dimension of life, all its theological principles are, nevertheless, constructed by human hands, and its social and ethical analysis is indistinguishable from that of the prevailing progressive rationalist orthodoxy of those who, like their forerunners since the eighteenth century, have been struggling to destroy the moral influence of the Church, in the face of all the results in human misery and the collapse of family life that their undoubted success has brought. 'If you can't beat them, join them': it is a principle that has taken over much modern theological endeavour, and certainly feminist theological endeavour. The systematic application of a secular 'feminist scale of values' as a yardstick to assess the acceptability of any specific part of the biblical revelation could hardly be outdone as an example of dedicated conformity to the world. And it is, above all, from the tortured and angry world of the secular feminist struggle that the 'feminist hermeneutics of suspicion' has been directly culled so that it may scatter broadcast its dragon's teeth of resentment and mistrust in the fertile soil of the Church's life. We have observed, again and again, how the Bible and the Christian tradition may be misrepresented, suppressed and distorted in order to assist the propagation of the primary feminist theory of the existence of a universal patriarchal conspiracy. But we are no longer concerned merely with a simple misrepresentation of facts. Rather, we are caught up as spectators at the birth of a fantastic new world. As Professor Fiorenza tells us, 'feminist analysis and consciousness raising enables one to see the world and human lives, as well as the Bible and tradition, in a different light and with different "glasses".'[40] Now, seen through the intervening lens of feminist consciousness, dreams become nightmares, and things which are honourable, things which are lovely, things which are of good report are suddenly, at a stroke, horribly changed, perceived by this new 'mind-set' as part of a vast tissue of lies and oppression. The effect of this distorting lens, applied by religious feminists to their perception of the Christian tradition, has been to produce a reversal of understanding of an extent unavailable to any merely secular feminism. What, for instance, does a major and respected Christian feminist like Rosemary Ruether think that husband and children and faithfulness within Christian marriage mean to a woman? What is the Church's tradition? Apparently this: marriage for the wife means that

> Only the male to whom she has been legally handed over may put his seed in her body, so that he can be sure that the children that emerge from her body belong to him, pass on his name . . . Man gives birth to woman, she is his offspring and creature, formed from his side to serve him in lowliness . . . the power of her motherhood is stolen from her, and she is reduced to an instrument of his virility.
>
> The Christian church teaches that birth is shameful, that from the sexual libido the corruption of the human race is passed on from generation to generation. Only through the second birth of baptism, administered by the male clergy, is the filth of mother's birth remedied and the offspring of the woman's womb made fit to be a child of God . . . Woman must subject herself to necessity, for this is the divine will. She must obediently accept the effects of these holy male acts upon her body . . .[41]

Is it really to be guilty of androcentric bias to suggest that such a blind and loveless apprehension of the reality of Christian teaching is so grotesquely and so evidently far from the truth as it has been lived through the ages, so clearly the product of a distorted 'historical imagination' formed in bitterness and resentment, that our main problem is no longer the apologetic one of reasoned counter-argument, but the more urgent pastoral task of judging how influential such writing may be, and containing the hatred and destruction it can surely cause? For, let there be no doubt, books such as Ruether's and Fiorenza's form part of an increasingly powerful cultural offensive, affecting not the Christian Church only, but western society as a whole. Former activists such as Germaine Greer,[42] Mary Kenny,[43] and Betty Friedan may now be having their doubts; but the movement as a whole is gathering rather than losing momentum. The devaluing of the family and the domestic arena (partly the root cause of modern feminism, but also later accelerated by it) and the irruption into the public arena of a large number of intelligent and educated women have created a dynamic which is far from exhausted, and which is no longer satisfied with the old goals. There is, in the words of the sociologist, Brigitte Berger, 'a new imperialism':

> The general acceptance of the feminist definition of private and public life in the Western democracies as the new orthodoxy, in conjunction with the prescriptive thrust of feminism, result in the feminization of politics, the feminization of the economy and the feminization of the culture. Taken together we may thus speak of the ascent of a new sentimental imperialism. This is carried, in the main, by the feminist vision that seeks to radically transform world culture. There are significant indications available to us today that this general imperialistic thrust of feminism is likely to be with us for some time and will decisively shape the direction of future public debates.[44]

It is clear that this new imperialism has been reflected in the life of the Church, too, and there are some reasons to suppose that its effects could well be more profound and more lasting even than its effects on the secular culture. Berger was writing in the autumn of 1983, at a time when the influence of the liberal intelligentsia (such indispensable allies of the feminist cause during the seventies) had in some ways been - temporarily no doubt - reversed, at least in the secular world. In the Church however, this influence remained as strong as ever. And though the Church is often resistant to change, this property does not always act to protect its life from undesirable encroachments; once changes are actually made, especially after a long period of agitation, the Church's natural tendency is to consolidate them quickly so as to avoid the upheaval of their reversal. The increasing momentum of the secular feminist movement, combined with the fixed belief of many Christian leaders that they acquire relevance to the world by reflecting its ever-changing assumptions as soon as these may be ascertained, could well, for large parts of western Christendom, be decisive. Unless, that is, a greater understanding is generally achieved of the truly revolutionary character of the reorientation which lies beyond certain immediate goals (most notably the ordination of women to the priesthood) which can so plausibly be represented as mere reformist adjustments. One thing seems certain: the more powerful the Christian feminist movement becomes, the more abundant will be the Church's bitter harvest of division, anger, suspicion and all uncharitableness.

NOTES TO PART FOUR

1 *The Penguin Complete Novels of George Orwell* (London 1983), p. 917.
2 Brigitte Berger and Peter L. Berger, *The War over the Family* (London 1983), p. 48.
3 Betty Friedan, *The Feminine Mystique* (London 1965), p. 13.
4 G. K. Chesterton, *What's wrong with the World*, (London 1910), pp. 149-50.
5 ibid., p. 128.
6 ibid., p. 121.
7 Esther Vilar, *The Manipulated Man* (London 1972), pp. 15-16.
8 Arianna Stassinopoulos, *The Female Woman* (London 1973), p. 115.
9 ibid., pp. 115-17.
10 Betty Friedan, *The Second Stage* (London 1982), p. 44.
11 M. Hutaff (ed.), *Woman and Roman Catholic: is it Possible*, Boston Women's Ordination Conference, Spring 1980, pp. 55-6.
12 ibid., pp. 56-7.
13 Publisher's blurb, back cover.
14 Elisabeth Fiorenza, *In Memory of Her* (London 1983), p. 41.
15 ibid., p. xiv.
16 ibid., p. 61.
17 ibid.
18 ibid.
19 ibid., pp. 61-2.

20 Orwell, op. cit.
21 Fiorenza, op. cit., p. 62.
22 ibid.
23 ibid., p. 61.
24 ibid., p. 68.
25 ibid., p. 60.
26 Rosemary Ruether, *Sexism and God-Talk* (London 1983), p. 94.
27 ibid., p. 95.
28 ibid.
29 See Mary Daly, *Beyond God the Father* (Boston 1973), p. 3.
30 ibid; also Ruether, op. cit., p. 96.
31 Stephen B. Clark, *Man and Woman in Christ* (Ann Arbor 1980), p. 319.
32 Mary Daly, *The Church and the Second Sex* (London 1968), p. 52.
33 Daly, *Beyond God the Father*, op. cit., p. 3.
34 Daly, *The Church and the Second Sex*, op. cit., p. 53.
35 *De Cultu Feminarum*, II, 1.
36 *Ad Uxorem*, II, 9.
37 *De Trinitate*, XII:VII:10.
38 See Niceto Blazquez, 'Feminismo Agustiniano', *Augustinus*, XXVII, March 1982, p. 11.
39 ibid., p. 52 (translated for the author by Henry Everett).
40 Fiorenza, op. cit., p. xxiv.
41 Ruether, op. cit., pp. 260-1.
42 Interviewed by Frances Cairncross for the *Guardian*; quoted by Mary Kenny, 'In the Driver's Seat', *Encounter*, LX (no. 2, February 1983), p. 29.
43 ibid., pp. 25-30.
44 Brigitte Berger, 'The emerging Role of Women', *Focus*, VII, (1983), p. 14.

Index

Index

Acknowledgements

Quotations from *An Inclusive Language Lectionary: Readings for Year A*, copyrighted © 1983 by the Division of Education and Ministry of the National Council of the Churches of Christ in the USA, are used by permission.

'For the Unknown Goddess' by Elizabeth Brewster is reprinted from *In Search of Eros* by permission of Clarke Irwin (1983) Inc. Copyright © 1974 by Clarke, Irwin & Company Limited.

Extracts from *Image-Breaking, Image-Building* by Linda Clark and others are reprinted by permission of The Pilgrim Press. Copyright © 1981 by The Pilgrim Press.

Extracts from *Man and Woman in Christ* by S.B. Clark are reprinted by permission of Servant Publications. Copyright © 1981 by S. B. Clark.

Extracts from *Beyond God the Father* by Mary Daly are reprinted by permission of Beacon Press. Copyright © 1976 by Mary Daly.

Extracts from *In Memory of Her* by Elisabeth Schüssler Fiorenza are reprinted by permission of SCM Press. Copyright © Elisabeth Schüssler Fiorenza 1983.

Permission to reprint extracts from *Womanspirit Rising: A Feminist Reader in Religion*, ed. Carol P. Christ and Judith Plaskow, has been applied for from Harper & Row Inc.

Extracts from 'God the Mother', a programme in the 'Credo' series *Behind the Veil*, first broadcast by London Weekend Television on 14 March 1982, are reprinted by permission.